HARVEST

HARVEST

Unexpected projects using
47 extraordinary garden plants

STEFANI BITTNER & ALETHEA HARAMPOLIS
Photography by David Fenton

TEN SPEED PRESS
Berkeley

FOR OUR GIRLS

FOREWORD

I once believed that clipping branches and blooms to bring indoors was akin to denuding my garden. But about ten years ago, I began to interview America's flower farmers and their customers—floral designers devoted to and creatively fueled by domestic and local botanicals. Mesmerized by their uncommon floral crops, I began to regard the incredible beauty of my own backyard for all of its potential. That meant enjoying not just the small quantity of food (berries, herbs, and vegetables) that my kitchen garden produced, but appreciating its abundance by displaying garden greenery and flowers in my vases.

This new-old philosophy of living with my garden's generous harvest is best learned from true practitioners, such as Stefani Bittner and Alethea Harampolis of Homestead Design Collective. These women are also proponents of good design, and they adhere to the guiding philosophy of choosing plants at once both ornamental and useful. Although not farms by any means, our urban and suburban backyards should be used in their entirety, say Stefani and Alethea. The culinary world has its own "nose-to-tail" way of eating, and *Harvest*, the book you hold in your hands, introduces the gardener's version of that

idea—call it a "fruit-to-root" way of growing— with an appreciation for all parts of the plant, from the first tender shoots in spring to the pods and hips of late fall.

I've learned so much from these two pioneers. Stefani is a role model for landscape designers, inspiring her harvest-minded clients to turn their once-unproductive yards into prolific (and lovely) sources of edible bounty. Alethea is a role model among the farmer-florist crowd, blending edibles with ornamentals, aromatics with the wild foraged, houseplants with weeds—all to create dramatic, moody, seasonal florals for everyday decor and magnificent occasions.

In *Harvest*, they celebrate the Slow Food movement on a highly personal scale, integrated with a Slow Flowers ethos. When edibles meet botanicals, we live intentionally with plants throughout the seasons. And when you embrace this practice, you will be richly rewarded by your garden.

Nothing is more local, more seasonal, or more sustainable than using what we grow. This is the central message of *Harvest*. The forty-seven plants and their accompanying projects recommended by Stefani and

Alethea will inspire you to grab your trowel and head straight to the garden. Why rely on the supermarket or big-box store for a centerpiece? The ingredients are at your fingertips in all four seasons, whether they be twigs and boughs in winter or lush summer blossoms. Mark the seasons with creativity, inspired by the garden. Feed yourself and your household in inventive ways. Those efforts also benefit nature around you, ensuring that wildlife sips at the nectar cup, pollinators find food, birds nibble on seeds, and beneficial creatures thrive.

After I became enthralled with (or, to be truthful, I fell down the rabbit hole of) the world of flower farming, I never viewed a cut flower without considering who grew it and where it was grown. I don't want flowers from halfway around the calendar year, not to mention halfway around the globe. And there is no reason you should, either.

I wrote a book about this concept, *The 50 Mile Bouquet*, suggesting that, as we do with our food choices, we should source our flowers close to home. Now, equipped and inspired by the wisdom of Stefani and Alethea, you can create a "five-step bouquet" that is truly seasonal and local, a reflection of your own relationship with the ground on which you live. Eat, smell, touch, and see the beauty of your harvest—and feel all of your senses.

DEBRA PRINZING, author, speaker, podcaster, and creator of Slowflowers.com

INTRODUCTION

Harvest is a practical, inspirational, and seasonal guide to living with an edible landscape. In this book, you'll find ways to make your garden more productive and enjoyable with a variety of projects using unexpected and often well-known garden plants, some of which may already be growing in your garden. Discover the surprising usefulness of petals and leaves, roots, seeds, and fruit. Turn turmeric root into a natural dye and calendula into medicinal oil. Use lilacs to create sweet-smelling cream and apricots to create a facial mask. Use crabapple branches to create stunning floral arrangements, oregano flowers to infuse vinegar, and edible chrysanthemum to enliven a salad. The plants in this book are not only remarkably useful, but they make for stunning additions anywhere in your garden. You'll find something exciting to harvest and create from one growing season to the next.

A garden is an extension of your living space. It should reflect your style and be a place where you want to spend time. A garden can benefit and enrich your life in so many ways. Yes, of course, there is the kitchen garden, where you grow annual herbs and vegetables. But we want to inspire you to grow harvestable plants throughout your entire landscape. This means growing edible plants that provide flowers, fruits, and herbs for use in the kitchen as well as throughout your home in beautiful arrangements. And just because a garden is beautiful doesn't mean it cannot also be useful.

THE PLANTS & PROJECTS
The plants and projects in this book are divided into three gardening seasons: early (late winter to spring), mid (summer to early fall), and late (late fall to early winter). These are flexible guidelines—the months that an individual plant is harvestable will vary depending on your climate and location. For us, *early* begins in the later stages of winter and early spring. For others, it may begin in midspring. But no matter where you live, you can adapt these seasonal designations to fit your area's climate and USDA hardiness zone, the standard by which gardeners can determine which plants are most likely to thrive in a location. We've included annual and perennial plants that grow in all zones. To determine what USDA hardiness zone your garden is located in, see page 209.

Some plants may be familiar, while others might surprise you. Many of the plants are so versatile they can be used in multiple projects. (See Project Ingredient Alternatives on page 204.) Once introduced, we hope that you will be inspired to learn even more about these plants on your own.

The plants and projects were photographed outdoors in our gardens over the course of a year and a half. You will experience the seasons as you read through the pages of this book, and, because of this, we share the plants in order of their harvest to use for projects, and not according to type.

We encourage you to use this book as a guide to choosing plants with seasonality in mind. Your garden has the potential to provide year-round harvests; you simply need to include plants that provide them. Use succession planting (see page 207) with early-, mid-, and late-season harvest times. In this way, just as one harvest ends, the next one begins. This is what distinguishes edible gardening from farming and will provide you with smaller, continuous harvests throughout the year.

FOOD SAFETY

As exciting as it is to grow food throughout your landscape, growing edible plants with common sense and food safety in mind is paramount to healthy living.

Have your soil tested. What a plant eats, we end up eating, so if our plants are grown in contaminated soil, we're exposed to the contaminants as well. If your home is older (pre-1978), it may have lead paint in its past. Likewise, if a fence is constructed of pressure-treated wood (made with arsenic), surrounding soil might include some heavy metal contamination. Designate these spots as places for nonedible plants.

Choose food-safe materials (natural wood and ceramics, for example) for growing containers, and avoid planters with possible toxic stains or paints. Finally, if you have pets, create a separate space in your garden for them so that they are not potentially contaminating your edibles.

ORGANIC GARDENING & BENEFICIAL INSECTS

Organic gardening and food safety go hand in hand. As with other contaminants, when your food plants are exposed to toxic pesticides, those pesticides end up in what you harvest and eat. If you are not already gardening organically, this is your opportunity to learn and implement organic gardening practices and principles.

One major principle in organic gardening is the need for beneficial insects and pollinators—and flowers to attract them. The great news is that the flowers we love to bring indoors to fill our vases and garnish our salads are the same flowers that pollinators and beneficial insects love, too. All of the flowers included in this book are edible, but feel free to fill your gardens with nonedible flowering plants as well. They create fantastic cut flowers and contribute to a beautiful landscape.

The ability to grow food throughout your landscape is one of the most exciting realizations a gardener can make. And when you make this happen, all kinds of other amazing things follow.

EARLY

These plants begin the garden's new year in late winter and spring. Early spring is a time for fresh, bright, chartreuse greens; tender new shoots of delicate herbs; and flowering branches filled with fragrant blooms. Once the garden wakes up, it explodes with growth and color: the deep reds of rhubarb stalks, the scent of lilac blooms, the colorful highlights of abundant breadseed poppies, and the endless flowers of black cumin. This is the time to fill your table and kitchen with flowers! Edible flower-pressed cheeses, the season's first pickles, and our first herb salads are just a few of our favorite ways to celebrate spring at the table.

RHUBARB
Rheum rhabarbarum

──────

You can save space in your kitchen garden for annual vegetables by planting rhubarb in the landscape mixed with other plants. The lush, crinkly green foliage atop rosy red, pink, and green stalks lends a tropical ambiance to any garden.

IN THE GARDEN

Rhubarb can be grown as an herbaceous perennial in USDA zones 3 to 8 and as an annual in other climate zones. Truth is, most of us can grow it anywhere for at least one season. It's a tough plant that can thrive on a fair amount of neglect, which is perfect for the busy home gardener, and it requires low water once established. Plants grow 24 to 48 inches (60 to 120 cm) tall and require full sun to partial shade in the ground or in a container.

Depending upon the kind of rhubarb you choose, stalk colors range from green to pink to red. Our hands-down favorite is 'Glaskin's Perpetual'.

On the greener side, it offers a tangy flavor and long harvest time. In fact, it is the only rhubarb that can be harvested throughout the growing season, hence the name.

HARVEST

Harvest only firm stalks, avoiding the late-season squishy stalks. Our preferred method is to grab the base of the rhubarb stalk and pull it away from the plant with a gentle twist. This technique typically removes the entire stalk, but if it doesn't, you can use garden shears to cut the stalk at the base of the plant. Always leave at least four stalks per plant to ensure continued plant growth. If not used right away, the stalks can be stored in the refrigerator for up to 3 weeks. Be sure to discard the leaves because they contain high amounts of oxalic acid and are considered toxic. Use your harvests to make preserves, compotes, cobblers, stews, shrubs, syrups, and, of course, a classic strawberry-rhubarb pie.

SMALL-BATCH, QUICK-PICKLED RHUBARB

Pickling in small batches is the way to go. Use the small quantities that a home garden provides rather than bulk amounts you schlep home from the farmers' market. The process is quick and easy, and it yields delicious results.

Pickled rhubarb stalks are a fun and unexpected addition to a cheese plate and add a delightful tang to roasted meats and veggies. Truth be told, our hands-down favorite way to use this versatile pickled treat is in cocktails. Try a stalk as a fanciful, flavorful swizzle stick for your next Bloody Mary.

MAKES TWO 12-OUNCE JARS

4 large rhubarb stalks, cleaned and trimmed

2 teaspoons peppercorns

½ teaspoon cloves

3 dried bay leaves

2 dried chiles

1 cup apple cider vinegar

1 cup water

1 cup organic sugar

½ teaspoon kosher or sea salt

Rinse the stalks thoroughly and cut them into 2- to 3-inch (5- to 8-cm) pieces or longer, depending on preference and jar size, and place in canning jars. Divide the spices and chiles evenly and add to the jars with the stalks.

In a small, nonreactive saucepan, combine the vinegar, water, sugar, and salt. Bring the mixture to a boil while stirring to dissolve the sugar. When the sugar is dissolved, remove the pan from the heat. Using a funnel, pour the liquid mixture into the canning jars over the stalks. Close the lids immediately, let the jars cool, and place them in the refrigerator.

Allow the rhubarb to pickle for up to 48 hours before serving. Quick pickles last up to 2 weeks in the refrigerator.

BREADSEED POPPY
Papaver somniferum

————

The breadseed poppy is considered the baker's flower because of its edible seeds. A key player in any garden, this prolific, colorful bloomer signals the arrival of spring. One glance of those gorgeous floppy, paper-thin blooms and striking seedpods, and you immediately understand their allure.

This poppy has a dark side due to its other common name (opium poppy) and the fact that every part of this plant is toxic except for the seeds. It's perfectly legal to grow this poppy for ornamental and culinary use, but obviously should not be grown for any illicit reasons.

IN THE GARDEN
This annual poppy can be grown in all USDA zones, in full sun and with moderate water. Plant poppies in herb and cut-flower gardens. At 24 to 36 inches (60 to 90 cm) tall, breadseed poppies are also perfect in large planting beds, where they provide a pop of color. Self-sowing and deer resistant, they convey a dreamy, carefree quality when mixed with ornamental grasses in a meadow-inspired design.

The seeds need light to germinate. When directly sowing, lightly press the seeds into the top inch of loosened soil rather than covering the seeds with soil.

HARVEST
As petals fade, large seedpods are revealed. Allow the poppy to complete its full life cycle on the stem, leaving the seedpod intact to mature and dry in the garden. Harvest seeds when the pods are dry and plump, and they rattle when gently shaken. Cut the poppies stem by stem, turning over each pod and pouring the seeds into a clean, dry jar. Dry seeds keeps for at least a year when stored in a sealed container.

A tasty addition to baked goods and salads, poppy seeds pair well with lemon in muffins and cakes. Use them to garnish pasta dishes and fruit salads. After harvesting the seeds, save the pods to use in dried flower arrangements or wreaths.

POPPY SEED DRESSING

MAKES ABOUT 1 CUP

1 small shallot

¼ cup champagne
vinegar

1½ tablespoons
poppy seeds
(from 3 to 5 flowers)

½ teaspoon kosher
or sea salt

½ teaspoon ground
mustard

½ cup good-quality
olive oil

One of the best ways to use your harvest is also one of our
favorites. This salad dressing pairs well with the delicate
seasonal greens and herbs of spring.

————

Peel and finely chop the shallot and place in a medium bowl. Add the
vinegar, poppy seeds, salt, and ground mustard. Whisk to combine.
Continue to whisk as you pour the olive oil into the bowl in a slow
stream, until completely combined. Store refrigerated in a sealed
container for up to 2 weeks.

LILAC

Syringa vulgaris

————

With its sweet, distinct scent, lilac is the fragrance of spring. But did you know that it's also edible? We love it so much that we recommend planting early-, mid-, and late-blooming varieties, which will give you four straight months of flowers and bountiful harvests.

IN THE GARDEN

Lilac is a perennial shrub that needs full sun and cold winter nights for successful blooming. Hardy in USDA zones 3 to 7, the sturdy lilac can survive in temperatures as low as −40°F (−40°C)!

We tend to place lilacs in the landscape as supporting shrubs, and never in a starring role. This is because once the blooms have faded (in a few short, glorious weeks), the lilac is an unadorned plain green shrub. Plant them along a sunny fence or in a mixed perennial bed as a foundation planting. Lilacs are quite carefree as long as they have full sun, good drainage, fertile soil, and once-a-year pruning.

Remove suckers (new stems that emerge from the base of the shrub) and any intersecting branches in the spring immediately after blooms fade. Use garden shears to cut out misshaped or crossing branches. If unpruned, they can reach 7 to 10 feet (2 to 3 m) tall. To control height, prune back stems by one-third. Lilac blooms on old wood, so it's important to prune the shrub at this time. If you prune later in the summer, you may remove a branch where the buds will later set.

HARVEST

Harvest lilac flowers in the morning and place the stems directly into a bucket of cold water. Harvesting in the afternoon sun will cause the flowers to wilt prematurely. Bring the bucket indoors, and place the flowers in a vase out of direct sunlight. Lilac blooms do not last long once cut. Cut branches can be used in arrangements, and the flowers are delicious in spring salads and as a gorgeous, delightfully scented garnish for baked goods and cocktails. Or use them as the basis for perfumed flower cream.

LILAC FLOWER CREAM

An ancient French technique, *enfleurage* is the process of extracting a flower's perfume into odorless animal or vegetable fat. The process used here is a simple method that will capture the fragrance of spring in a jar. The cream can be used directly on your skin or to flavor favorite sweet dishes. It is best to use the lilac's tiny blooms straight from the shrub, picking them in the morning when they are the most fragrant.

———————

Pick 2 cups of lilac blooms. Place the coconut oil in a small saucepan and melt over low heat until it is completely liquefied. Pour the liquid into a 10 by 10-inch (25 by 25-cm) casserole dish and allow it to harden. After the oil has hardened, score it with a butter knife. This will help the scent of the flowers penetrate it more deeply. Layer the tiny lilac blooms onto the oil, covering it with 2 inches (5 cm) of blooms. Place a second 10 by 10-inch (25 by 25-cm) casserole dish upside down atop of the first one. Use electrical tape to seal the two dish edges tightly, and place the dishes in a dark area.

After 48 hours, remove the tape seal and discard the spent blooms. Pick another 2 cups of lilacs, add another 2 inches (5 cm) of flower blooms to the oil, and seal again for another 48 hours. Repeat this process three more times, for a total of five cycles with fresh blooms each time.

MAKES TWO 16-OUNCE JARS

32 ounces extra-virgin coconut oil

10 cups lilac blooms picked from the heads in 2 cup increments as needed

Scrape up the oil from the casserole dish, place it into two 16-ounce jars, and seal the lids. Store in a cool, dark place; the flower cream will keep for up to 3 years.

APPLE & CRABAPPLE
Malus spp.

Nothing beats a fresh apple plucked from the garden. The taste of a homegrown fruit is far superior to anything you'll find at the supermarket, because home apple varieties are selected for flavor, not shipping quality.

If you have room in your garden for another fruit tree in the same genus, one that's also highly ornamental, we enthusiastically recommend crabapple. In the spring, it pops with amazing blooms that ultimately reward you with small fruits in the fall that can be used for pickles, jelly, or cider.

IN THE GARDEN

Apples are long-lived trees in USDA zones 4 to 10. If planted in full sun with regular water, they reliably send out beautiful blooms in the spring, with late summer and fall fruits that are loved by everyone. Several apple varieties are touted for their special uses (such as baking and cider), but don't let this stop you from eating them fresh and on their own.

With so many apple varieties to choose from, we encourage you to seek out local heirloom varieties for your own favorites.

When planting multiple fruit trees, think in terms of succession planting (see page 207). This is easy to accomplish, because apple varieties have a wide range of ripening times, from midsummer through late fall. With a little planning, you can harvest fresh apples for about five months.

HARVEST

When apples seem ripe and ready to harvest, pick one and cut it in half. The fruit should be firm to the touch. Take a bite and sample the flavor. If the flesh is tinted green or tastes exceedingly tart, they may need more time on the branch. You can also take a look at the seeds, which are brown when the fruit is ripe.

Although few things beat the fresh taste of an apple straight from the tree, use your late-winter prunings to create branch-based arrangements.

BRANCH ARRANGEMENT

Fruit trees need to be pruned in late winter or early spring (see page 207). We like to prune our apple and crabapple trees in early spring, after the branches are budded up and even beginning to bloom. We use these branches in arrangements as the first apple and crabapple harvest of the year. The crock (or vase) and arrangement will be heavy, so you may want to work where you will be placing the final arrangement.

Fill a large crock, vase, or vessel with clean, cold water. Take the branches and remove any leaves or flowers that might fall below the water line. This will keep the water clean and allow the arrangement to last longer. Prune off any dead or damaged twigs, leaves, or blossoms.

3 to 5 pruned, flowering apple or crabapple branches of varying lengths

Cut off the bottom inch of the tallest branch and add it to the left side of the vessel. Continue trimming and adding branches, cutting some shorter to make the arrangement more dimensional, so that not everything is at the same level and height. Alternate placement on the left and right sides of the vessel. Using this technique, you can build a web of stems inside the vessel that will help the branches stay in place and not fall over. The smaller branches should gradually arch out and away from the tallest branch in a natural, asymmetrical pattern. Allow some of the blossoms to hang below the lip of the vessel.

BACHELOR'S BUTTONS
Centaurea cyanus

———

One of our favorite edible flowers, bachelor's buttons' tiny petals remind us of confetti. Pull the petals from the center of the flower and use them as a pretty garnish for anything from soft cheeses and salads to cakes and cocktails.

IN THE GARDEN

An annual flower, bachelor's buttons thrive during the cool season as well as during the warmer midseason months. In hotter climates, they perform best in light to partial shade. Plants tolerate a wide variety of soils with good drainage. Regular watering is recommended, but plants can handle some dry spells.

Deer tend to resist it, and pollinators can't stay away from it. Plant single-color varieties in a mass for big visual impact in planting beds, or combine them with other edible flowers such as German chamomile, borage, and yarrow in the kitchen garden. The gray-green foliage mixes well with other flowers, making it a lovely addition to cut-flower gardens and containers.

We prefer the taller kinds, at 24 to 36 inches (60 to 90 cm). Our favorites include the nearly black blooms of 'Black Gem', the deep blue 'Blue Diadem', and the bright red blossoms of 'Red Boy'.

Deadhead (remove) spent flowers for a new flush of blooms, but allow a few to go to seed so that they can self-sow for the following year. In areas with mild winters (such as USDA zones 7 to 10), the seed can be sown in fall for early-season flowering.

HARVEST

Although bachelor's buttons look great in the garden, they are quite fun in the kitchen, too, plus they make charming cut flowers, fresh or dried (see page 206). When the weather is warm, harvest flowers in the morning to avoid wilted blooms. Choose flowers that are just opening and avoid those that are spent (the older, wilted blooms). Dried flowers can be added to tea blends, and fresh flowers can be used in salads, in dyes, and, as you're about to find out, for transforming plain butter into something brilliantly festive.

BLOOMING BUTTER

A stick of butter and a few flowers are the basis for this beautiful and delicious way to preserve your edible flower harvest. Compound butters (mixtures of butter, flowers, and herbs) can be prepared and frozen for up to 6 months. We like using bachelor's buttons because the tiny petals are the perfect size and require no additional chopping. If you are growing more than one variety of bachelor's buttons, use them all. Add a bit of the flower-flecked butter to grilled fish, flank steak, or grilled vegetables. For equally delicious variations on this recipe, substitute chives for the shallot.

MAKES 4 OUNCES

10 to 12 bachelor's button flowers (¼ cup); use more or fewer petals, depending on how "confetti-fied" you want your butter to be

4 ounces butter, softened (not melted)

1 teaspoon lemon juice

½ teaspoon lemon zest

1 medium shallot, diced

Gently rinse the flowers and set them aside to dry on a clean cloth. Stir together the softened butter, lemon juice, lemon zest, and shallot. Pinch the petals from the flowers, discarding the bitter-tasting centers. Add the petals to the butter mixture and stir.

If using immediately, store the butter on the kitchen counter, away from heat. To preserve the butter, roll it into a log shape (or multiple small rolls that can be used as needed), wrap it in parchment and then foil, and freeze. The butter will keep for up to 6 months. When you're ready to use it, let the butter come to room temperature before serving.

SALAD BURNET
Sanguisorba minor

———

Salad burnet is a member of the rose family (Rosaceae). Its early, lacy foliage bridges the gap between winter and summer leafy herbs, offering the taste of cucumber well before the actual cucumber harvest season arrives.

IN THE GARDEN

We plant salad burnet along pathways for easy access, because we love to snack on it while we work. Don't be fooled by its delicate appearance—this is a hard-working plant. Perennial in USDA zones 4 to 8, it can be harvested until the first snowfall. Plants grow 15 to 35 inches (38 to 90 cm) tall and spread to about 12 inches (30 cm). These drought-tolerant plants will grow in most soils, though they prefer moist soils and sunny conditions. They tolerate partial shade but not full shade, making them a great planting under a fruit tree.

Salad burnet is easy to grow from seed, or you can transplant plants as seedlings, though it is a bit more complicated when it comes to reproduction. The plants are hermaphrodites that produce male and female flowers. The flowers are not self-pollinating and pollen must be distributed by wind, bees, or other insects for the plants to reproduce. When they're successful, watch out! Salad burnet will reseed and freely produce new plants.

HARVEST

As with any leafy plant harvest, do not harvest salad burnet in the high heat of the day or you'll be left with a handful of wilted greens. Harvest in the cool of the morning or evening instead. Rinse the leaves in cold water and use a salad spinner to dry them. Use the greens immediately or store them wrapped in a clean towel or storage bag in the crisper section of your refrigerator. Salad burnet typically lasts a week or two in the fridge.

Salad burnet is the basis for spring herb salads and makes a great vinegar infusion. Try adding a bunch of finely chopped leaves to crème fraîche–based dips for a delicious cucumber flavor kick. Add a few leaves to your mixed garden salads, enjoy with sliced melon, or use it instead of mint in sparkling water and cocktails.

EARLY-SEASON HERB SALAD

Salad burnet tastes like spring. We use it in our spring herb and edible-flower salads, including this one, a favorite homegrown preparation. This savory standout herb salad will not keep, so harvest only the amount of salad burnet that you need. Here's a good rule of thumb: A handful of herbs equals one serving, so if you're serving four people, you will need at least four handfuls for your salad.

_____

Rinse the herbs in a bowl filled halfway with cold (not warm) water. Gently swish the herbs in the water to loosen any dirt or lingering insects, lift the herbs out, and place them in salad spinner. Give the herbs a gentle spin, and then lay them on a clean cloth. Herbs must be sufficiently dry because the vinaigrette will not adhere to wet leaves.

Gently chop the herbs and place them in a salad bowl. Drizzle the vinaigrette over the herbs, sprinkle with salt, and gently mix. Remember to go lightly with the vinaigrette to avoid limp herbs and petals. Remove the petals from the edible flowers and add them to the salad bowl after the greens are dressed. Alternatively, the flower petals can be added to individual plates before serving. Serve immediately.

SIMPLE CHAMPAGNE VINAIGRETTE

MAKES ¾ CUP

½ cup extra-virgin olive oil

½ cup champagne vinegar

In a bowl, whisk together the oil and vinegar. Store in a sealed container for up to 2 weeks refrigerated.

MAKES 4 SERVINGS

4 handfuls of garden herbs, such as salad burnet, chervil, flat-leaf parsley, French sorrel, mint, nasturtium leaves, and peppermint candy flower leaves

Simple Champagne Vinaigrette (recipe follows) or Poppy Seed Dressing (page 14)

Kosher or sea salt

5 to 10 stems of freshly harvested edible flowers, such as bachelor's buttons, borage, calendula, and nasturtiums

ARTICHOKE & CARDOON

Cynara scolymus & C. cardunculus

———

Did you know that when you're eating an artichoke, you're eating a thistle? Same goes for its cousin, the cardoon, although its leaf stalks are more edible. No matter how you eat them, this prickly, tasty pair adds welcome drama to the garden with their silvery gray ornamental foliage and striking flowers.

IN THE GARDEN

Artichokes and cardoons can be grown as perennials in USDA zones 7 to 10 and as annual plants in all other zones. Requiring low water and full sun, artichokes and cardoons have an upright, columnar growing habit up to 5 feet (1.5 m) tall and 4 feet (1.2 m) wide, with lobed, serrated green foliage and thistlelike flowers. Artichoke flower heads are larger than those of cardoons, and their nearly spineless leaves are less divided in shape. The large, unopened flower bud of the artichoke includes the leaflike bracts and heart, both of which are edible. If allowed to remain on the stalk, artichoke and cardoon flower heads

open to large, spectacular violet-blue flowers and are no longer edible.

Although we love the classic green globe artichoke, the more unusual purple artichokes are beautiful additions to the garden. Seek out artichokes 'Carciofo Romanesco', 'Opera', 'Violetta Precoce', and the 'Imperial Star', an early producer and great choice for cooler climates. Also look for the unusual red-purple–tinged cardoon, 'Rouge d'Alger'.

HARVEST

Harvest of both plants begins early. For cardoons, the most tender stalks, which taste a bit like celery, should be harvested in spring before the plant flowers. Artichoke heads also form in spring and are easy to harvest. Simply cut them off the stalks before they bloom. We prefer to harvest as we go, leaving the flower heads on the plant until we're ready to eat them. What we do not use in the kitchen, we let bloom for use in arrangements.

ARTICHOKE ARRANGEMENT

Artichokes are a favorite edible, but few know that their layers of prickly leaves can also be used to create a beautiful focal point in a mixed garden bouquet. Bring inside in a few cuttings from the garden to make a stylish and simple composition.

––––––––

Fill a large crock or vase with clean, cold water. Remove any damaged leaves from the stems or leaves that would fall below the water line. Add the large artichoke heads in the front of the crock, with one head resting slightly higher than the other. This creates a focal point and showcases the gorgeous multilayered leaves.

2 large artichoke heads, stems and leaves attached

Add in the smaller artichoke stems to the back and left sides of the crock. These heads should sit taller than the larger heads. They add height to the arrangement and create an asymmetrical look. Add in some of the wild carrot stems to fill in the space between the larger and smaller artichokes. These stems should be slightly taller than the small artichoke stems. Place the remaining carrot stems on the back right side of the crock to complement the wild carrot on the left and provide an airy backdrop to the arrangement.

1 or 2 stems with several small artichokes attached

5 to 8 stems wild carrot flowers (*Daucus carota*), 12 to 18 inches (30 to 46 cm) long

2 nasturtium vines with flowers, each 12 to 18 inches (30 to 46 cm) long

Add the longest nasturtium vine to the front side of the crock, to the left of the large artichokes, so that it drapes over the side of the crock. This creates movement and softens the edge of the vessel. Use the other nasturtium vine to fill any gaps. Make sure that the flower heads are turned to be visible from the front of the arrangement.

PEPPERMINT CANDY FLOWER
Claytonia sibirica

This pretty cousin of miner's lettuce (*Claytonia perfoliata*), peppermint candy flower, also known as pink purslane, has gorgeous foliage and adorable candy-striped flowers. Peppermint candy flower shines when planted under large perennials or in the shady corner of a vegetable garden. Easy to plant by seed or transplanted as seedlings, this edible perennial will bloom all spring and summer long.

IN THE GARDEN
Hardy in USDA zones 3 to 8, the perennial peppermint candy flower grows to 8 inches (20 cm) tall in full shade, partial shade, and sun in nearly any soil. Its versatility makes it a go-to plant for problem spots in the garden.

The plant's appearance is reminiscent of its cousin, wild miner's lettuce, that's typically found in woodland settings. With its soft leaves, it's not surprising that peppermint candy flower thrives in a moist environment, but, surprisingly, it can also thrive in dry conditions. You'll want to harvest and enjoy peppermint candy flower often, so make sure to plant it in a spot where you can easily access its leaves and flowers.

HARVEST
Harvest full stems in the cool of the morning to avoid wilted greens. This sturdy perennial can last up to 2 weeks refrigerated. You can use peppermint candy flower in a variety of ways. The succulent leaves have a mild, neutral taste that's perfect for homegrown salads. The greens can also be cooked and are a great addition to other braising greens. Sprinkle the sweet flowers over salads, use them as a garnish, or press them into cheese.

EDIBLE FLOWER-PRESSED CHEESE

Flower-pressed cheeses make great host gifts and party appetizers. They are simple to assemble in just a few minutes.

MAKES ONE 4-OUNCE ROUND OF CHEESE

5 to 7 peppermint candy flower stems, each with multiple flower heads

4-ounce round of fresh goat or other mild soft cheese, such as sheep

Fruit, poppy seed crackers, or a baguette, for serving

Rinse the flowers in a bowl filled with cold water by gently dipping the flowers to remove any debris. Lift out and place on a clean, dry towel. Remove individual flower heads from the stems and gently press into the cheese round in any pattern you choose. You can also use the mild-tasting leaves and stems to create patterns with the flowers.

Serve immediately with fruit, poppy seed crackers, or a sliced baguette, or wrap the cheese with wax paper and store for up to 3 days in the refrigerator.

ELDERBERRY

Sambucus spp.

———

The great thing about growing elderberry is that you can harvest both the flowers and the fruit. When eaten, the sweet elderflower has hints of vanilla and is popularly used in everything from cordials and tinctures to infusions and teas. And if you haven't tried elderflower tonic water in your gin and tonic, you must! To create infused tonic water, follow the recipe for Edible Flower—Infused Water (page 178), substituting tonic water and elderflowers for water and violas.

The blue-black elderberries are rich in medicinal properties and well known as powerful immunity boosters. They are chock-full of antioxidants and vitamins A, B, and C.

IN THE GARDEN

Elderberry is hardy in USDA zones 3 to 10. The large perennial shrub is right at home alongside other edibles such as apple and lilac. We often allow our elderberries to reach 8 to 12 feet (2.4 to 3.7 m) tall before pruning them to restrict growth. Deciduous and deer resistant, elderberries are considered low-water plants. In the first year of growth, however, they must be well watered to establish strong and shallow roots.

Elderberry attracts beneficial insects and other wildlife to the garden. It can grow in full sun to partial shade, though it produces less fruit in the shade. This versatility makes it an excellent shrub for repeating in the landscape. 'Black Lace' is particularly striking, named for its multiple stems that bear deeply incised, nearly black foliage. Pink buds morph into white flowers in late spring, followed by black fruit in autumn.

HARVEST

The edible components of elderberry are the flowers and ripe fruit. Do not eat the leaves, unripe berries, bark, and roots, however, because they are all toxic. Harvest elderflowers just before the shrubs are in full bloom (typically May and June). When harvesting, use both hands—one hand to clasp the flower cluster, and the other to snip the cluster free. To dry the flowers, place them on a towel in a warm, well-ventilated spot. When thoroughly dry, the little flowers can be rubbed off the umbels and stored in sealed jars in a dark place for up to a year. Be mindful of harvesting only some of the flowers early if you want to have juicy, delicious berries to eat later in the year.

Elderberry fruit normally matures in late summer to early fall. When harvesting the berries, always look for bunches that are completely black-purple, and skip the unripe little green berries. Look for clusters that have an elderberry "raisin" or two to help avoid other berries that haven't fully ripened. Destemming is a bit tedious but necessary. After washing, you can use elderberries right away or preserve them by freezing (for up to a year) or drying them in a food dehydrator. From fresh or dried elderflowers you can make syrup, tea, or infused honey or vinegar. Use the berries in wines, juices, and jams.

ELDERFLOWER-INFUSED HONEY

One of the easiest ways to preserve fresh elderflowers is by adding them to honey. The combination is an effective remedy for sore throats, early-season colds, and allergies. Add elderflower honey to tea or simply enjoy it by the healing spoonful. We mix it with fresh lemon juice and carbonated water for a refreshing lemonade.

Infusing elderflower into honey couldn't be easier, and this recipe is wonderfully flexible depending on the quantity of your harvest. You can use smaller or larger amounts of flowers and however much honey you have on hand. Choose the size of the jar to determine how much of the flowers and honey you'll need. You need only enough flowers to fill the jar loosely, followed by the honey, and then you'll be set to partake in the delicious results. Don't toss out extra flowers! Dry them and use them for tea.

———————

Rinse the flowers with water. Remove and destem the blooms from the branches and set aside. You should have a pile of lovely small, white flowers, free of bark, stems, and immature fruit.

Loosely pack the flowers into an 8-ounce jar with a lid and pour the honey over them. Use a chopstick or knife to stir the honey and elderflowers gently to release any trapped air and submerge the flowers in the honey. If needed, top off and fill to the brim with more honey. Secure the lid and set aside to infuse for 1 week.

MAKES 8 OUNCES

¼ cup (or more) freshly picked elderflower heads

8 ounces fresh local honey, or more as needed

Strain the elderflowers out of the honey using a small sieve, pouring the infused honey into a second clean jar and sealing with a lid. Store in a cool, dark place, such as a pantry, for up to 6 months.

BLACK CUMIN
Nigella sativa

———

Native to Asia and the Middle East, black cumin is an annual flower with lacy foliage; beautiful, delicate white blooms; and balloon-like seedpods. The seed capsules each contain five compartments, which, when dried, open up to disperse the seeds. Small, black, and tasty, the seeds are used as a peppery spice in Indian and Asian cuisines.

In addition to black cumin, *Nigella sativa* has numerous other common names: nutmeg flower, blackseed, black caraway, fennel flower, Roman coriander, and onion seed. It's also often confused with its popular cousin, love-in-a-mist (*Nigella damascena*), which has a similar look but whose seeds are not typically eaten.

IN THE GARDEN
Our love for black cumin stems from its effectiveness as a successional annual bloomer throughout the early and midseasons. In warmer climates, sow seeds once a month, from just before the last frost of spring until late summer, and then once again near the end of autumn for early spring crops. This will result in a prolonged blooming period—spring through autumn.

Sow seeds directly by covering them with light soil, keeping them moist until germination. Plants grow 8 to 12 inches (20 to 30 cm) tall and can be transplanted easily. Although the plant prefers well-drained soil, it's not fussy and is known to grow in most conditions. This versatility makes it an easy choice for full-sun meadow plantings or cottage and herb gardens.

HARVEST
If you don't pick the flowers, they will eventually turn into wonderful showy seedpods. Harvest the tasty seeds just as you would poppy seeds (see page 13). Sprinkle the seeds on your favorite Asian-inspired dishes and salads. Use the seeds for tea, or add them to coffee for a boost of spicy flavor. Black cumin's delicate blooms also make a beautiful contribution to a fresh or dried flower arrangement.

WARMED OLIVES WITH BLACK CUMIN SEEDS

Black cumin seeds are used as a remedy for everything—except death. Their amazing healing powers have helped people with ailments ranging from diabetes to high blood pressure to colon cancer. Toasting the seeds and serving them with warm olives is a great way to reap their benefits, and it makes an elegant nibble for get-togethers and cocktail parties.

————

MAKES ABOUT 3 CUPS

¼ cup extra-virgin olive oil

Strips of zest from 1 small lemon

3 cups mixed olives, such as Castelvetrano, kalamata, niçoise, and Cerignola

2 tablespoons black cumin seeds

Salt and pepper

In a medium saucepan, combine the olive oil with the lemon zest and olives, and heat for about 6 minutes over low heat. In a separate dry pan, toast the black cumin seeds over low heat for 5 minutes, stirring frequently. Pour the warm olive oil, zest, and olives into a bowl and sprinkle the black cumin seeds over the top. Season with salt and pepper. Serve warm.

FEVERFEW

Chrysanthemum parthenium

———

Feverfew is a traditional medicinal herb historically used to treat a variety of conditions, including migraine headaches, arthritis, and, as its name implies, fever. It is also a beloved garden plant appreciated for its easygoing nature and boundless small, white, daisylike flowers. Whether your interest lies in its medicinal value or simply its decorative qualities, feverfew can be a welcome addition to the garden.

IN THE GARDEN

Feverfew resembles and is often mistaken for chamomile, but feverfew has more a vertical growing habit, reaching 24 inches (60 cm) tall, with lacy foliage and long, thin stems. This member of the aster family (Asteraceae) has been grown in herb and medicinal gardens for centuries. In USDA zones 5 to 9, it can be grown reliably as a perennial, but it works as an annual in other zones. Sprinkle the tiny seeds in the garden in early spring, but don't cover them with soil because they need sunlight to germinate. For best flowering, feverfew requires full sun, although it will grow in partial shade. It is relatively carefree and can thrive in poor soils with moderate amounts of water.

Feverfew contains pyrethrin, a natural insect repellent that gives the plant its distinctive scent. Some would describe it as citrusy, others bitter. Do not place feverfew near plants that need pollination because bees dislike the aroma. On the other hand, feverfew can also keep pests away, so consider using it as a companion plant for roses or other pest-prone botanicals.

Frequent cutting of blossoms helps the plants stay in bloom longer, encouraging new growth. When grown as a perennial, feverfew can be cut back to the ground after frost. It reseeds easily, so deadhead spent flowers to control unwanted self-seeding. Try some of our favorites: 'Aureum' (golden feverfew), with its finely cut, chartreuse-yellow foliage; 'Plenum' (plenum chrysanthemum), which produces showy, larger flower heads; and 'Tetrawhite', with clusters of little double-white daisylike blooms.

HARVEST

Harvest leaves and flowers to use for medicinal and ornamental purposes. Feverfew's anti-inflammatory properties make for great essential oils or salves to help soothe sore muscles, joint pain, and arthritis. Once dried (see page 206), use the leaves and flowers to make tea and tinctures to relieve headaches and muscle pain. You can harvest large bunches to make a kitchen wreath. Don't use the leaves while they are still fresh, however, because herbal experts advise that they are more likely to trigger an allergic reaction for sensitive folks.

FEVERFEW TEA BUNDLES

We hang bundles of feverfew and other herbs to dry to make a delicious mixed-herb tea. Feverfew's tiny blooms pack a wallop of healthful vitamins, such as vitamins A and C, as well as iron and niacin. As its name suggests, feverfew can be used to relieve high fevers; it also helps dull a painful migraine and eases anxiety with its earthy fresh aroma, which pairs perfectly with mint and rosemary. Stems for the bundles should be 8 to 10 inches (20 to 25 cm) long. One of our favorites, feverfew tea is simple to make.

Cut about 3 feet (1 m) of kitchen twine into three 12-inch (30-cm) pieces. Cut another piece of twine about 3 feet (1 m) long. Attach the long piece of twine to a place where it can hang free. (We use a doorway in the pantry.)

Create three bundles of herbs using four stems each of the feverfew and mint, and two stems of rosemary. Wrap a small piece of kitchen twine several times around the stems at the base of each bundle and tie to secure. Leave 3 inches (8 cm) or more free to use to attach the bundle to the hanging twine (the longer piece you cut).

Attach the three herbal bundles to the hanging twine, spacing them about 4 inches (10 cm) apart. This will enable air to circulate around the bundles so they dry completely and don't mold. Let the bundles dry for 2 to 3 months.

When the bundles are dry, crumble together the dried herbs from all of the bundles over a large bowl. Use these dried leaves to create tea in a French press or tea ball to steep. Fill one-half of a tea ball for an 8-ounce cup of tea. The dried herbs can be stored in a sealed jar at room temperature for up to 1 year.

**MAKES 3 BUNDLES
AND ABOUT 3 CUPS
OF DRIED TEA**

12 stems feverfew

12 stems mint (any
available varieties)

6 stems rosemary

APRICOT
Prunus armeniaca

———

The apricot stands gracefully among our favorite fruit trees, and with good reason. It bears sweet, aromatic fruit early in the growing season; provides shade during midseason; and has gorgeous foliage color in the fall.

IN THE GARDEN

A low-water fruit tree, apricot is the first to bloom and the first to harvest in early-season gardens in USDA zones 4 to 9. Many varieties are self-pollinating, so you don't need to plant more than one apricot tree for it to produce fruit. Different types of apricots require different chill hours (see page 207) to produce fruit, so choose one that matches your climate. Plant apricot trees in a sheltered location protected from strong spring winds that could blow off their flowers—no flowers means no fruit. We also advise planting later-fruiting apricots such as 'Katy' if you experience late frost or spring winds in your area.

Because branches can easily break with the excess weight of too many fruits, thinning the fruit is a necessity. If you don't thin, you risk losing an entire tree limb full of fruit. Simply hand-twist the smaller, unripe fruit until it detaches from the branch. Remove young fruit (smallest is best and perhaps least heartbreaking) every 2 to 4 inches (5 to 10 cm) along each branch.

Apricot looks beautiful in a cottage, traditional, modern, or Mediterranean garden. We find it striking enough to be a front-yard focal-point tree, and several different types of apricot can work wonderfully together in the landscape to produce fruit throughout the summer (see Succession Planting, page 207). We're huge fans of 'Blenheim', the cold-hardy 'Harcot', and the late-fruiting 'Autumn Glo', all of which produce fantastic fruit.

HARVEST

Pluck your homegrown bounty when the fruit is soft and easily detaches from the tree. The fruit ripens all at once, so you will have plenty of fruit for a couple of weeks and then none at all. Off the tree, apricots last about a week on the counter or stored in the crisper section of the refrigerator if the fruit becomes overripe. Although we eat as many fresh apricots as we can, there are many ways to maximize the yield: you can preserve, candy, or dehydrate your harvest, or create syrups, cocktail infusions, and homemade beauty products.

APRICOT FACIAL MASK

High in vitamins A and C, apricots are a nutritious snack, but they are also a wonderful treat for your skin. We eat our way through the harvest but save some fruit to create this relaxing facial mask. The natural fruit acids gently exfoliate dead skin cells, while the vitamins help rejuvenate the skin surface.

As with any face scrub, apply the apricot cleanser no more than once or twice per week. If you have extra, store it refrigerated in an airtight container and use it within 3 days—or, better yet, share some with family and friends.

MAKES 1 CUP

5 apricots, pitted and peeled

½ cup warm purified or filtered water

1 tablespoon organic whole milk

1 tablespoon raw honey

Combine all of the ingredients in a blender and blend until smooth.

To apply, remove any makeup and rinse your face with warm water. Avoiding the eye area, spread the mask over your face and neck. After 15 to 20 minutes, rinse with warm water.

MID

Summer to early fall is a time of abundance, with the arrival of many edible flowers and herbs. Long, hot days mean sweet fruits, iced tea, and cocktails, including concoctions that use edible flowers in vinegars and spirits. The food and arrangements are simple and clean, as the harvests do not need embellishing.

SCENTED GERANIUM
Pelargonium spp.

_____

No herb or cut-flower garden is complete without scented geranium. From foliage texture to fragrance, its diversity is astounding. Leaves range from smoothly rounded to finely cut and lacy, with colors ranging from gray to green. But it's really all about the scent—no other plant boasts so much aromatic variety.

IN THE GARDEN

Scented geranium can be grown as a perennial in USDA zones 8 to 11. Elsewhere it can be grown as an annual or taken indoors for the winter if it's grown in containers. Plants grow 24 to 36 inches (60 to 90 cm) with a 12- to 24-inch (30- to 60-cm) spread and require full sun to part shade and moist soil.

Whether in the garden or in a container, make sure your scented geraniums are within easy reach, because the plants' fragrance is released by gently rubbing the leaves. Plants offer a wide variety of scents: rose, fruit (including all citrus), nut, mint, and pungent. There are more than 250 varieties of scented geranium, and most gardeners have a few favorites. They come in many shapes, colors, and fragrances. In the landscape, we particularly love *Pelargonium tomentosum* 'Chocolate' and 'Peppermint' for their large, fuzzy leaves and sprawling growth habit. The low, dense foliage of 'Nutmeg' makes it a great choice for edging a scented pathway. Mix *P. crispum* 'Variegatum', the variegated lemon geranium, with grasses and perennials in planting beds for a burst of fragrance, color, and texture. 'Skeleton Leaf Rose' and *P. graveolens* often make their way into our herb and container gardens.

HARVEST

Freshly harvested scented geranium leaves are a delightful addition to a salad or a glass of iced tea. Or add them to jams, flavored sugars, syrups, and honey. Citrus-scented varieties are known to repel mosquitoes; try rubbing a leaf on your skin as a natural mosquito repellent. The leaves can be dried (see page 206) to retain their scent for years and then used for home or body fragrance. Newly picked stems can be steeped in bathwater to infuse it with a wonderful, natural perfume. Just as we love the beautifully textured foliage in the garden, we appreciate it in our bouquets as well.

SCENTED GERANIUM SUGAR

Long used by bakers the world over, herbal sugars are easy to make and yield exciting flavors. They also provide a fantastic means of preserving your scented geranium harvest. Even sweeter is that the sugar lasts indefinitely, so you can use it for a special occasion or when fresh ingredients are not available.

There are two basic techniques for preparing herbal sugars. One involves adding the dried herb leaves whole to the sugar for some period of time and then removing them. The other requires that the dried leaves be minced and mixed with the sugar. This recipe uses minced leaves, resulting in a visually and aromatically pleasing sugar speckled with the tiniest pieces of geranium foliage.

Use your taste buds to guide you in your scented geranium choice. Lemon-scented geraniums are particularly versatile and are a natural to include in cocktails. Try *Pelargonium crispum* or 'Bitter Lemon' or 'Frensham Lemon'.

For flavoring the rim of a glass of pear brandy or other favorite liqueur, gently rub a slice of lemon on the rim of a cocktail glass. Dip the glass in a bowl of the geranium sugar, rotating it to be sure a generous amount adheres to the rim. The lemon juice and sugar will crystallize, creating a "rock candy" effect on the glass, which imparts each sip with a deliciously sweet, citrusy taste.

MAKES ½ CUP

5 to 7 fresh scented geranium leaves

½ cup high-quality organic cane sugar (do not use fine baker's sugar)

Destem the geranium leaves, rinse them in cool water, then lay them on a towel to dry. When completely dry, place leaves and sugar in a food processor. Gently pulse until leaves are minced. Transfer the mixture to a dry, clean jar and seal. (If the sugar hardens, give the jar a good shake before using.)

OREGANO
Origanum vulgare

This culinary classic is at home in every garden. Its wonderful wandering habit makes it a natural for cascading over walls and filling in pathways. Plant it within reach for easy harvest.

IN THE GARDEN

Oregano grows easily in USDA zones 4 to 9 as a perennial, and as an annual in other areas. This is a Mediterranean plant that you can stress out—it enjoys full sun and spots in the garden that receive less irrigation. For everyday use in the kitchen, Greek oregano (*Origanum vulgare* var. *hirtum*) is our favorite, reaching about 24 inches (60 cm) at maturity. Use dwarf Greek oregano (such as *O. vulgare* 'Compacta Nana'), a mounding oregano that spreads 24 to 36 inches (60 to 90 cm), for border plantings in the vegetable garden. The variegated 'White Anniversary' sprawls beautifully in all of our herb gardens and often in our planting beds. Golden oregano (such as 'Aureum'), at 12 to 36 inches (30 to 90 cm), puts on a gorgeous show with small chartreuse leaves. Golden crinkled oregano (such as 'Aureum Crispum') adds texture to rock garden plantings.

We love the lesser-known Syrian Za'atar oregano (such as *O. syriacum*) that is prevalent in Middle Eastern cuisine. Its grayish leaves and upright growth habit, to 36 inches (90 cm), make for a beautiful addition to our herb gardens and container plantings.

HARVEST

Harvest stems throughout the growing season to dry and preserve. If the oregano is growing as an annual, harvest the whole plant before the first frost and dry for use later (see page 206). Because oregano comes from the mint family (Lamiaceae), notorious spreaders, it needs to be harvested often to keep it under control. If growing it in a raised planting bed, place it along the edges and let the plant cascade over the sides.

Harvest the interior growth so that the plant does not overtake prized planting space. There's no need to harvest it all before it flowers because the bees love it. In fact, oregano is our number-one plant in the kitchen gardens we design not only because it's stunning and tasty but also because it lures all sorts of pollinators. Oregano blooms bring texture and fragrance to a homegrown herb bouquet and boost the flavor profile in salads and infusions.

EDIBLE FLOWER-INFUSED VINEGAR

Oregano blooms enliven vinegar with a delicate tint and a distinctive flavor. Oregano-infused vinegar is destined to be your new favorite for making some of the best-tasting vinaigrettes you've ever had. Oregano possesses strong, natural antimicrobial properties, so vinegar infusions made from the herb can be taken at the onset of winter colds and respiratory infections. If you have backyard chickens, add a few drops of the herbal infusion to their water feeder for a healthy flock.

Champagne vinegar is used here because its light taste complements and does not overwhelm the delicate nature of the oregano flowers. You can use this vinegar in all of your favorite vinaigrette recipes.

MAKES 2 CUPS

1 cup fresh oregano flowers and leaves, removed from stem

2 cups champagne vinegar

Gently rinse the herbs, checking for any hitchhiking pests and debris. Then dry the blooms and leaves thoroughly on a clean towel. Fill a 16-ounce jar with the flowers and leaves, and pour the vinegar on top. Seal with a lid and store in a cool, dark space. Check the mixture periodically and give the jar a good shake if any of the flowers or leaves have floated to the surface.

After a week, strain the vinegar into a clean jar, discarding the oregano flowers and leaves, and seal with a lid. Store in a cool, dark place, such as the pantry, for up to 1 year.

LAVENDER
Lavandula spp.

One of the most recognized scents in the world, lavender generously offers many culinary, medicinal, and decorative uses. The flowers are the fragrant foundation of our garden bouquets. In the kitchen, we use it to flavor salt and sugar, to brew tea, and to make aromatic simple syrups for sodas and cocktails.

IN THE GARDEN

Most types of lavender grow well as low-water, full-sun perennials in USDA zones 8 to 11. In other areas, it is well worth growing as an annual. Our favorites are high in essential oils. We use *Lavandula* × *intermedia* 'Provence' (24 to 36 inches, or 60 to 90 cm, tall and wide) for covering large swathes in a landscape, and the compact *L. angustifolia* 'Hidcote' (12 to 18 inches, or 30 to 46 cm, tall and wide) along pathways or under roses, where its deep-colored blooms can be appreciated.

For a touch of the unexpected, we plant the variegated and aromatic 'Meerlo' (24 to 36 inches, or 60 to 90 cm, tall and wide) in containers. If you're growing lavender as a perennial, shear it to a ball shape when it's dormant in the late winter season to avoid an overly woody base, which results in a leggy or scraggly looking plant. If a woody base does develop, it's best to replace the entire plant.

HARVEST

If you're harvesting to make lavender bundles or sachets, do so when the plant is full of buds and the flowers have barely opened. If you're using it to make an essential oil, harvest full stems, including leaves and flowers, because the essential oils are derived from both. The flowers and leaves can be dried (see page 206) and used in everything from bath products and sachets to delightful desserts and soothing teas.

LAVENDER & MINT TEA

MAKES 2 CUPS

10 to 15 (or more) fresh or dried lavender flowers

4 to 5 freshly harvested mint stems, such as chocolate (*Mentha × piperita* 'Chocolate') or red stemmed (*Mentha × gracilis* 'Madalene Hill')

2 cups boiling water

Combine lavender with chocolate mint leaves for a soothing, yet invigorating, tea.

————

Gently rinse off any dirt or insects from the lavender and mint with cool water. Place the flowers and mint leaves into a teapot. Pour the boiling water over the lavender and mint, and let steep for 15 minutes. For a stronger tea, allow it to sit for another 5 minutes. Sip and enjoy.

ALPINE STRAWBERRY
Fragaria vesca

Alpine strawberry is one of our go-to edible groundcovers, and with good reason. This well-behaved plant stays put rather than sending out runners and taking over your garden. Its fruit rarely makes it inside because we cannot stop ourselves from snacking on them in the garden. The petite bite packs a wallop of sweetness, and plants produce berries continually throughout summer and fall. Yellow and white varieties are our trusted favorites, because they fool birds and raccoons into thinking the fruit is not yet ripe, leaving more for us.

Alpine strawberry also scores major style points for its numerous ornamental possibilities. It drapes beautifully from window boxes and containers, it looks handsome as an edging plant along a garden path or flower border, and it is equally at home in a rock garden or woodland setting.

IN THE GARDEN

Hardy in USDA zones 4 to 8, alpine strawberry grows 1 to 4 inches (2.5 to 10 cm) tall. It thrives in full sun and, unlike most strawberries, grows in partial shade as well, though it bears less fruit if it does not get enough light. The smaller fruit (¾ inch, or 2 cm) does not require full sun to be sweet, which makes it an excellent option for planting it under fruit trees and shrubs. Plant in fertile, moist, well-drained soil near pathways for easy harvest. Because it is a short-lived perennial, it will need to be replaced every four years or so.

HARVEST

Our favorite way to eat alpine strawberry is simple: freshly plucked from the garden. Though they produce fruit all summer long, production peaks in midsummer. Pick and enjoy them when they turn a deep red; or for non-red varieties, fruits should give slightly to the touch. Use any fruit that you haven't devoured after harvest to make a wonderful jam or to add sweetness to any beverage or cocktail infusion.

What most folks don't know is that the flowers and leaves have edible properties, too. Use the flowers to make a sweet, small bouquet. Fresh or dried (see page 206), the foliage can be steeped for a lovely tea. Add a handful of blossoms and fruit to desserts, salads, and drinks.

ALPINE STRAWBERRY & FRIENDS POSY

1 stem foxglove,
10 inches (25 cm) long

2 stems flowering
basil, 10 inches
(25 cm) long

2 stems *salvia lyrata*,
10 inches (25 cm) long

2 stems black cumin
flowers, 8 inches
(20 cm) long

2 stems scented
geranium, 8 inches
(20 cm) long

2 stems anise hyssop,
8 inches (20 cm) long

7 stems alpine
strawberry, including
fruits and leaves, cut
as long as possible

We like to pick flowers and create posies while walking through the garden. A little snip here and there of several plants, flowers, and herbs are easy to assemble in hand, and there's really no wrong way to put it together. Tie varying lengths of stems together with a piece of vintage ribbon to create an even prettier bouquet.

————

Cut 12 to 18 inches (30 to 46 cm) of ribbon. Lay all the materials flat on your work table to organize them for assembly.

Gather the longer-stemmed items first, such as the foxglove, basil, and salvia, loosely in your left hand. These will be used for the back side of the posy. Add the black cumin, geranium, anise hyssop, and strawberry stems (making sure the fruit is visible) on top of the longer stems in your hand. Place the geranium leaves on top of the bunch in hand to create a full posy shape.

Attach a rubber band at the bottom of the stems to secure them, and then cut all the stems at once so that they are even at the bottom. Tie the ribbon around the rubber band to cover it, wrapping the ribbon around twice; tie it with a bow or knot of your choice.

PURPLE CONEFLOWER
Echinacea purpurea

Echinacea is a popular medicinal herb that earned its fame as an herbal preventative for warding off winter colds. In the garden, the large, conical seed head in the middle of the showy flower resembles the spines of an angry hedgehog (hence the name: *echinacea* means "hedgehog" in Greek).

IN THE GARDEN

Native to the United States, purple coneflower is hardy in USDA zones 3 to 10 and can be grown in forty-nine of the fifty states—even southern Alaska. Reaching 24 to 36 inches (60 to 90 cm) tall, echinacea performs best in full sun to part shade, with moderate water in well-draining soil. Bees, butterflies, and hummingbirds cannot resist the flowers, which bloom early summer through late fall. Deer tend to leave it alone.

Echinacea are what we like to call "perennials, with an asterisk." We have tried many varieties that do not reliably return the following year. Even the more reliable species of *E. purpurea* plantings need to be freshened up with supplemental plantings in the spring. Still, they are well worth growing. Just know they can behave a bit like annuals, so enjoy those that return and treat any that survive the winter as a bonus.

There are many ways to enjoy this beautiful medicinal in the landscape. Use it in planting beds, herb gardens, cut-flower gardens, meadows, orchards, and containers. It's stunning when combined with other edible flowers and when planted alone en masse. We love mingling echinacea with ornamental grasses, yarrow, calamintha, oregano, basil, and so much more. After the last fall blooms fade, do not deadhead the plants; leave the seed heads on the plants for continued winter interest.

HARVEST

The medicinal qualities of echinacea are most often obtained from its roots. As gardeners, we want the plants (and thus do not harvest the roots), so instead we recommend harvesting and using the petals and dried seed heads. Dried flower petals (see page 206) can be used for teas and salves, and the seed heads are beautiful in dried arrangements and wreaths.

GARDENER'S SALVE

Simple, effective, and useful medicines, echinacea salves can soothe minor sores, wounds, insect bites, and stings—perfect for the home gardener. To create this recipe, you'll need to have already created an essential oil using echinacea flowers. Follow the recipe for Calendula-Infused Essential Oil (page 202), substituting echinacea for the calendula.

———

Place the beeswax in a medium, nonreactive saucepan and pour in the infused oil. Gently warm the mixture over low heat until the beeswax melts. Stir the mixture, and when the beeswax and oil are thoroughly combined, pour the mixture into jars and seal with a lid.

Place the jars in the refrigerator for 10 to 15 minutes to determine their solidification. The consistency of salves can easily be adjusted depending on your preferences. Once cooled, you can make adjustments by adding more oil (for a softer salve) or more beeswax (for a firmer salve) and warming the mixture again. The salve should last up to 6 months when stored in a cool, dark place.

MAKES ABOUT 1 CUP

1 ounce beeswax

1 cup echinacea-infused essential oil

ANISE HYSSOP
Agastache foeniculum

Every garden should include anise hyssop! This plant gives and gives at every stage of its life—from the edible flowers and seeds to the aromatic leaves.

Anise hyssop is the most culinary member of the *Agastache* genus. We plant it along trellises to attract pollinators to annual vegetables, in herb gardens to add height with its beautiful spike of purple flowers, and in perennial beds mixed with other low-water edible flowers such as feverfew, echinacea, and bee balm.

IN THE GARDEN
Requiring full to part sun and little water, and adaptable to most soils, anise hyssop is easy to grow by seed or transplant, reaching 24 to 48 inches (60 to 120 cm) tall and 12 to 24 inches (30 to 60 cm) wide. Try it as a perennial in USDA zones 4 to 9 or as a worthy annual in other areas. In the spring, we find new self-sown transplants growing throughout the garden, some volunteering in the crevices of planting beds. We'll leave some where they wander and dig up others and plant them where we want a pop of color.

In warmer climates, anise hyssop sends up a second harvest of blooms in late fall to early winter if spent blossoms are cut back in the summer. The plant is deciduous and will die back when frost hits, but it will reliably reemerge the following spring.

HARVEST
Harvest leaves from early spring through fall as needed to add a hint of licorice flavor to herb salads, cocktails, and delicious iced tea. Early-summer and late-fall blooms can be used as a garnish.

ANISE HYSSOP ICED TEA

Anise hyssop tea is one of our favorite summer drinks. On hot days, it is incredibly refreshing and the subtle, smooth licorice taste is sweet all on its own without any added sweetener. Loved by Native Americans, this plant is said to relieve a dispirited heart, and can sooth the pain from coughing when you have a chest cold. A few stems added to a French press with boiling water is all you need to experience its benefits.

MAKES 8 CUPS

5 to 8 anise hyssop stems, plus additional leaves and flowers for garnish

8 cups boiling water

Ice cubes

Gently rinse the plant parts with cool water to remove dirt and debris. Fill a large French press halfway with the anise hyssop (leaves, stems, and flowers). Add the boiling water and let steep for 15 to 20 minutes. Carefully press down the plunger. Pour the tea over ice into a pitcher or glass. Garnish with anise hyssop leaves and flowers to serve.

BLUEBERRY
Vaccinium spp.

With its delicious fruit and year-round ornamental beauty, the blueberry is one of the most beloved plants in the edible landscape. In fact, we think it's a great problem solver in the garden. Shallow roots enable it to be planted in tight spaces, and its roots won't compete with tree roots. Two basic types of blueberries are commonly available: the highbush blueberry (such as *Vaccinium corymbosum*) and the lowbush, or wild, blueberry (such as *V. angustifolium*). The first step in blueberry planting is choosing the type that grows best in your climate.

IN THE GARDEN

This long-lived perennial shrub can be reliably grown in USDA zones 4 to 10. Both types of blueberry will happily grow in full sun to part shade, making them easy to include throughout your garden. Although there are self-pollinating varieties, blueberries bear more and bigger fruit when grown with a friend. In other words, plant at least two blueberry plants to allow for cross-pollination. For success with blueberries, soil is more important than climate. They require a soil that is moist, acidic (pH 4 to 5), high in humus, and heavily mulched to moderate moisture levels. They require regular water and will not thrive in a low-water landscape.

The highly ornamental blueberry serves many purposes. Evergreen varieties make excellent screening and hedging plants. Deciduous varieties are prized for the fall color they bring to planting beds as well as their gorgeous, bell-shaped flowers in white, pale pink, or red, sometimes tinged in green. Blueberries also make stunning container plants and are excellent when several varieties are planted to produce fruit throughout the season. Plant early-, mid-, and late-season varieties to ensure a continuous harvest.

Highbush blueberries are probably the best known and are the type typically sold in nurseries. The name "highbush" comes from their vertical growth habit, at 6 to 8 feet (1.8 to 2.4 m). Northern highbush blueberries (*V. corymbosum*) grow best in USDA zones 4 to 7, and southern highbush grows in zones 7 to 10, where they have low chilling requirements and high heat tolerance.

Lowbush blueberries (*V. angustifolium*) are exceptionally hardy (USDA zones 3 to 6), making them excellent choices for gardeners who live in areas where winter temperatures dip below freezing. The low-spreading deciduous shrub grows to 18 inches (46 cm) and makes a wonderful groundcover.

HARVEST

Blueberries don't achieve their full flavor and aroma until a few days after they turn blue. If they are plucked a little too early, they are tart and sweet, which we don't mind. One of the great rewards of growing your own food is that you can conduct your own taste test—in this case, eating the blueberries at different stages of ripeness to determine how you like them best.

BLUEBERRY DYE

Making dyes from your garden is a wonderful way to preserve the season's colors in your textiles. Unlike commercial dyes that use harsh and toxic chemicals, your homemade organic dye is safe and natural. The natural dye process is quite easy (see page 206 for basics), and once you have given it a try, your eyes will be opened to more of your garden's colorful possibilities!

When used as a natural dye, blueberries create the most beautiful range of summery blues and purples, like the color of your favorite faded blue jeans. Hues range from periwinkle to pastel blue, magenta, and deep purple. Good enough to eat, this dye will stain your hands, so be sure to wear gloves while working. Blueberry dye creates a color that's perfect for napkins.

————————

To prepare the fabric to accept the dye, mix the salt and water in a large stockpot and set over medium heat. Add the napkins and allow to simmer for 30 minutes. Remove the fabric, let cool to the touch, and wring it out. You'll be adding the wet fabric to the dye, so set aside.

To prepare the dye, in a large pot combine the blueberries and water and bring to a boil. Simmer for 1 hour. Or, to achieve a darker color, continue to simmer the blueberries for 2 to 3 hours. When the water is cool enough to touch, remove the blueberries from the dye using a strainer or your hands. (Make sure you're wearing gloves!)

FABRIC AND FIXATIVE
½ cup table salt

8 cups water

6 white 100% cotton or linen napkins

BERRY DYE
2½ cups fresh blueberries

4 cups water

Add the wet fabric to the dye and simmer for about an hour for deep color. Remember that wet fabric always looks darker until it is rinsed and wrung out. Remove the fabric from the dye bath, rinse it with cold water until the water runs clear, wring it out, and hang to dry. Remember that the dye will drip from the fabric as it dries, so hang it in an appropriate place to avoid staining.

FLOWERING BASILS

Ocimum 'Dark Opal' × *O. kilmandscharicum* 'African Blue' and *O. basilicum* 'Wild Magic'

With spikes of gorgeous, fragrant flowers that range from dark violet-red to purple and white, these flowering basils are a showy, productive addition to the vegetable garden and attract pollinating honeybees. A bit milder than some other basils, with a hint of camphor, they bear an enticing fruity scent, and the taste of both leaf and flower has a distinct sweetness. Unlike the annual Genovese basil (*Ocimum basilicum* 'Genovese'), its Italian cousin, these purple-flowering basils are sterile; they have been bred to bloom and will continue to grow (rather than perish) while flowering.

IN THE GARDEN

Purple-flowering basils can be grown as a perennial in USDA zone 10 and as an annual in other areas. They are a bit more cold tolerant than many basils, and they usually last in our garden until first frost. Because these basils are sterile, they do not produce any seed and must be propagated from cuttings. You can take root cuttings before the first frost, grow them inside during the winter, and then plant them in the garden come spring. They are also fairly low maintenance, living on less water and fertilization than Genovese basil.

We plant 'African Blue' in sunny spots throughout our kitchen and cutting gardens, filling any needed space with this flowering beauty. 'African Blue' grows to 3 feet (1 m) tall and 2 feet (0.6 m) wide, so make sure to give this plant space. 'Wild Magic' tops off at 18 inches (46 cm) high, making it a perfect plant to edge a fragrant pathway.

HARVEST

Cut stems in the cool of morning and place them in water immediately; if the basil wilts, it does not reliably rehydrate. As long as it is not allowed to wilt, these basils can last for weeks in a vase. Do not store basil in the refrigerator because its leaves will wilt and turn black. The leaf flavor doesn't become bitter when flowering begins, as it does with other basils, so you can keep harvesting leaves and flowers all summer long. Use the leaves and flowers for garnishes, Caprese salad, herbal vinegars, and other favorite summer fare. Your harvests will be bountiful, so create fragrant arrangements to fill your home with sweet aroma.

FLOWERING BASIL ARRANGEMENT

It's no surprise that the fragrant blooms of flowering basils make for excellent garden bouquets. The key to creating a long-lasting basil arrangement is to harvest the flowers during cool mornings and keep the cut plants out of direct sunlight. Don't be surprised if the blooms start to root in the base. You can plunk them back in the ground if you're in a mild climate or in a small pot indoors. You will need waterproof floral tape and a 10 by 10-inch (25 by 25-cm) piece of chicken wire or a floral frog for this arrangement.

———

Fold a 10 by 10-inch (25 by 25-cm) piece of chicken wire into a ball shape and place it (or a floral frog) into the bottom of a large, low salad or soup bowl. Using waterproof floral tape, crisscross the tape above the wire ball in an X-shape across the bowl, securing the tape ends on the inside of the bowl. Fill the bowl with clean, cold water.

20 to 50 stems of flowering basil, 6 to 18 inches (15 to 46 cm) in length

Place the basil stems into the chicken wire, one stem at a time, grouping the shorter stems in the center of the bowl. Add the longer stems around the edges of the bowl for a draping effect. Continue adding in stems until the chicken wire is no longer visible.

GEM MARIGOLDS
Tagetes tenuifolia hybrids

These edible marigolds are covered in fragrant blooms from early summer until the fall. Low-mounding plants, their lacy foliage is pretty, but the abundance of flowers truly steals the show. Our favorites include 'Lemon Gem', 'Tangerine Gem', and the bicolor 'Red Gem'.

IN THE GARDEN

The gem marigold hybrids are full-sun annual bedding plants in all USDA zones. They tolerate heat and drought conditions and will bloom until the first frost. Their showy nature makes them an exceptional choice for borders, containers, and herb gardens, and they are conveniently sized (8 to 10 inches, or 20 to 25 cm) companion plants for tomatoes in a kitchen garden.

They also attract beneficial insects such as bees and hoverflies and have natural mosquito-repelling properties—plant them near gathering places for mosquito-free outdoor summer evenings. Deer are likely to leave them alone, too. Watch out for snails and slugs that can devour small seedlings; apply an organic slug repellent around the base of the plants, as needed.

Direct sow in spring after the last chance of frost. Plants germinate quickly (4 to 7 days). Deadhead the spent blossoms regularly, because the more you harvest, the more the plants will bloom. If plants get leggy, cut them back harder and they will reemerge in a bushier form.

HARVEST

Snip individual flower heads to garnish cocktails. The edible flowers can be used whole to infuse bitters (where their bitter centers are appreciated and needed), or separate the petals to sprinkle over a dish for an aromatic, colorful lift. Gem marigolds also create a beautiful dye for textiles.

MARIGOLD BITTERS (AMARO)

MAKES 1 QUART

Enough herbs and edible flowers to fill a 1-quart jar, for example:

- 1 cup gem marigold flowers and leaves
- 1 to 3 sage leaves
- 2 to 6 anise hyssop flowers and leaves
- 1 sprig rosemary
- 1 to 6 lavender blooms
- Small bunch of thyme (such as French, English, or lemon)
- 1 to 6 calendula flowers
- 1 to 6 bee balm flowers and leaves
- Small handful of rose petals
- 1 to 8 viola petals

5 to 10 alpine strawberries or other berries

Rind of 2 chinotto oranges

2 (750-ml) bottles Hangar One Vodka or a similar good-quality, unflavored vodka

SIMPLE SYRUP
MAKES ABOUT 1¼ CUPS

1 cup water

1 cup organic sugar

Amaro is an Italian herb-infused bitter liqueur, originally used as an after-dinner digestif, chilled or over ice. Recently, however, there's been a bitters revival, with cocktail enthusiasts mixing the bittersweet digestif into beverages beyond just classic cocktails such as the Manhattan and the old fashioned.

Gem marigolds are a perfect component because of their distinct bitter flavor and for the lovely amber hue that results. For *amaro*'s signature tartness, we've added some chinotto orange rind, the key ingredient in Campari, the popular Italian herbal aperitif.

————

Gently rinse the herbs and flowers, leaving the blooms intact to capture the bitter attributes of their centers. Add them all, along with the berries and citrus rind, to a 1-quart jar. Fill the jar with vodka to just below the rim (you might not need it all) and seal with a tight-fitting lid. Store it in a cool, dark place.

Check the *amaro* daily or every couple of days, and give it a good shake to ensure that there are no floating leaves or flowers. After 4 weeks, taste the *amaro*. If you prefer it stronger, allow it to infuse for another week or so. Once you've achieved the flavor you like, strain out the herbs, edible flowers, berries, and rind.

Next, make the simple syrup. Combine the sugar and water in a nonreactive pan. Place over medium-high heat and bring to a simmer, stirring to prevent sticking. Once the sugar has dissolved (about 5 minutes), remove the mixture from the heat and let it cool slightly.

Add 1 cup of the simple syrup to the strained *amaro* liquid and let infuse for an additional 2 weeks, then taste. If you find the *amaro* more bitter than you'd like, add more simple syrup but remember the sweetener is meant to take the edge off of the bitter taste rather than mask it. Once the bitters are to your liking, store indefinitely.

LEMONGRASS
Cymbopogon citratus

Lemongrass is a veritable feast for the senses. It tastes delicious, smells wonderfully lemony, feels good to run your hands through, and looks stunning in the landscape. Plus, as with many grasses, it can beautifully fill a patch of bare garden space.

Plant lemongrass within easy reach for cooking and in areas of the garden where you spend summer evenings, so you can take in its citrusy scent. Lemongrass contains citronella; run your hands through it to release natural essential oils that repel mosquitoes.

IN THE GARDEN
A subtropical plant, lemongrass is a perennial in USDA zones 9 and up. In zones 8 and lower, it can be grown as an annual or brought indoors to overwinter (see page 206). Lemongrass appreciates full sun and thrives in heat and humidity. It also grows well indoors and loves a warm greenhouse. The plant is considered mature and ready to harvest when it reaches 12 inches (30 cm) tall.

Lemongrass thrives in loamy soil and should be frequently fertilized with organic compost. It performs best with regular watering—it's difficult to overwater this plant. If you have a low-water garden, plant lemongrass in a container so that you can water it more frequently.

HARVEST
The stalk is ready to harvest when it's ¼ to ½ inch (0.6 to 1.3 cm) wide. Grasp firmly near the base of the stem and pull. Wrap stalks in a damp paper towel, place inside a plastic bag, and refrigerate for up to 2 weeks. Stalks can also be preserved by drying or freezing. Dry whole stalks in the dehydrator or slice them into ¼-inch (0.6-cm) pieces to freeze; they'll last indefinitely. The inner white core is used in cooking, but don't discard the leaves because you can use them to make a light, lemony tea. The whole stalk can be used to make a salt scrub.

LEMONGRASS SALT SCRUB

Lemongrass has antibacterial, antioxidant, and other therapeutic properties. After a hard day working in the garden, we appreciate lemongrass as a remedy for our aches and pains. Use this salt scrub on your hands daily or on sore muscles once a week while taking a deep soak in the tub. If you have very sensitive skin, you may want to use the salt scrub only on your hands or substitute brown sugar for the salt as a milder alternative.

MAKES ABOUT 1½ CUPS

1 or 2 fresh stalks lemongrass

1 cup sea salt

½ cup almond or olive oil

Finely chop the lemongrass by hand or in a food processor. Combine the chopped lemongrass, salt, and oil in a bowl and mix with a wooden spoon—or even better, use your hands. The texture should be moist enough to hold together but not overly oily. (If it does get too oily, add a pinch more salt.) Scoop the scrub into a 12- to 16-ounce jar and seal with a lid. Use within 2 weeks.

To use, simply spoon a small amount into your hands, gently rub it in, and then rinse your hands with warm water.

ROSE
Rosa spp.

Roses are a plant with emotive qualities. Many of us think of the varieties our grandparents grew, our first bouquet, the familiar fragrance. We love the wide variety of colors, scents, and tastes. Roses can fill so many spaces in the garden—as a groundcover, a shrub, or a climber. Rose petals have a slightly sweet, fragrant taste and add an unusual touch to desserts, infusions, and salads.

All roses have edible petals, but the way you treat and grow the plant determines whether or not its petals are safe to eat. Before you eat any part of the rose (or any plant), make sure that it has not been sprayed with chemicals or pesticides—this is why growing your own makes so much sense. If you have not transitioned your entire garden to organic care yet, roses are a good place to start.

IN THE GARDEN
Depending on the type of rose, it will prefer partial shade to full sun, though most roses prefer sunny conditions. These are hardy perennials and can survive in a variety of conditions. There are many different types to choose from so keep hardiness and growth habits in mind when choosing yours. You'll find a rose for most zones from USDA zone 3 and up.

Many roses have a single bloom season, while others bloom continuously throughout the season. Plant several types that will bloom in succession (see page 207), so that your roses will be in constant flower, from late spring to fall.

HARVEST
Pick roses in the morning before the heat of the day wilts the flowers. Flowers do not rehydrate well, so if you pick a wilted stem it will probably remain wilted. For arrangements and edible uses, pick flowers that are just opening, not the already open or spent flowers. Immediately place harvested stems in cool water and keep them out of direct sunlight. Uses include petal jam, vinegars, baked goods, teas, sorbets, beauty products, and cordials.

ROSEWATER FACIAL TONER

Rosewater is the perfect scent for a fragrance minimalist. Not only does it contain all of the medicinal benefits of roses, the water also takes on the wonderful scent of the flower as well. In addition to being an anti-inflammatory and a calming scent, rose is a natural cooling astringent with skin-soothing properties. This combination makes this rosewater facial toner a wonderful addition to your skin-care routine. Use daily by moistening a cotton pad or ball with a few drops of the rosewater and applying to your face.

————

Dip the roses in cold tap water to clean them, and remove the petals. Place a medium heatproof bowl upside down in the bottom of a large pot. Scatter the rose petals around the inverted bowl. Pour the distilled water over the petals, then place a second heatproof bowl on top of the first, right side up. Cover the pot with the lid placed upside down so that the handle of the lid is inside the pot.

Bring the water to a gentle simmer on the stove. When you see condensation on the underside of the lid, place a few ice cubes directly on top of the lid or on a dish towel on top of the lid; this helps attract the rose essence—filled condensation to the center of the lid, so that it can drip into the bowl. Continue simmering the petals until all the water has been collected in the top bowl, which can take about 45 minutes. (Be careful not to boil longer than this; the delicate essence can overcook or you can scorch the pan if the water boils out.)

Remove the top bowl from the pot. Carefully pour the hot rosewater from the bowl through a funnel into a sealable bottle or small jar. Be careful not to spill any of the precious essence. Your rosewater is ready to use! It will keep for up to 3 months.

MAKES 3 OUNCES

15 to 30 roses

3 cups distilled water

About 12 ice cubes

Strain the remaining petals from the water and collect any water left in the pan. The simmered water is darker in color than the essence, but it still smells wonderfully rosy. Add it to your rosewater or keep it separate and use it to flavor drinks or baked goods.

YARROW
Achillea millefolium

Although often planted as a flowering perennial, yarrow is a valuable herb for its durability in the garden as well as for its medicinal uses. Hardy and versatile with fernlike leaves and colorful blooms, yarrow has large, flat-topped flower clusters that are beautiful in the garden and as a cut flower.

The flower and the upper portions of leaf and stem are used as a natural remedy for colds and flu, but yarrow is perhaps best known for its antibacterial, anti-inflammatory, astringent, and analgesic properties. It's ideal for preventing infection, stopping blood flow, and reducing swelling and pain in wounds. Yarrow boasts several aliases—staunchwort, woundwort, nosebleed, knight's milfoil—all alluding to this herb's remarkable ability to stop a wound from bleeding while reducing pain and infection.

IN THE GARDEN

Exceptionally hardy, yarrow grows best in USDA zones 3 to 9. It thrives in full sun and isn't fussy about the soil it lives in. It performs well with low to regular watering and can tolerate poor soils on the drier side. It's also easy to grow from seed or transplant and can spread widely.

Plants grow on narrow stems, from 6 inches to 3 feet (15 cm to 1 m) tall, and flower clusters average about 3 inches (8 cm) wide, but sizes vary depending on the variety. Snip spent blooms throughout the summer to stimulate continuous blooming. In the fall, once yarrow is done flowering, simply cut back the spent blossoms, so that its beautiful lacy foliage can remain for winter interest.

Yarrow is the number-one attractor of beneficial insects to the garden. We have lots of favorite yarrows. Western yarrow (*Achillea millefolium* var. *occidentalis*) is excellent for medicinal purposes. For dried bouquets and wreaths, we prefer the silver-foliaged, yellow-flowering 'Moonshine', which retains its color even when dried. In a mixed perennial planting, we often use 'Pomegranate' for its neat and tidy vertical growth habit and deep-red blooms. With its pale-yellow flowers, the dwarf 'King Edward' makes a charming edging for a path or planting bed, while 'Apfelblüte' ('Apple Blossom') blushes with lovely soft pink tones.

HARVEST

The flowers and upper portions of the leaves and stems offer many medicinal uses, making yarrow an important herb in the medicinal garden. Harvest flowers as they begin to open, avoiding spent flowers. Snip full stems at the base of the plant to harvest both leaves and blooms. Create a poultice by macerating fresh flowers and leaves to create a compress applied directly to cuts and bruises; it also calms inflammation. And if you're feeling feverish, a freshly brewed cup of yarrow tea or tincture made from fresh leaves or flowers offers welcome relief.

YARROW HERBAL TINCTURE

Creating tinctures is a fun and easy way to include herbs in your life and preserve your herb harvest. A single drop of a tincture (dropped into a cup of warm water or applied under the tongue) can have the same soothing effect as a cup of herbal tea, but the concentrated tincture is more easily absorbed into the body.

The liquids most often used for a tincture base are high-proof alcohols such as vodka or brandy, or you can use apple cider vinegar. We used brandy for this tincture. Regardless of the alcohol chosen, it should be at least 80 proof (40 percent alcohol), which acts as a preservative to prevent any mildewing of the plant material in the bottle. To make a larger batch, use 1 part fresh herbs to 2 parts alcohol or cider vinegar.

MAKES 16 OUNCES, OR EIGHT 2-OUNCE GLASS DROPPER BOTTLES

1 cup freshly harvested yarrow leaves and flowers

2 cups brandy (at least 80 proof) or organic apple cider vinegar

Cut or tear fresh yarrow leaves and flower heads into 1-inch (2.5-cm) pieces and lightly pack them into a 16-ounce jar, filling it to just below the rim. Pour the brandy into the jar, to the top, to cover the yarrow. Secure with a lid and store in a dark, cool place.

In a day or two, open the jar and top off with more brandy to replace any liquid that has been absorbed by the yarrow. After 6 weeks, strain the tincture through cheesecloth over the opening of the jar into a glass measuring cup. Use a small funnel to pour the tincture into small glass dropper bottles. Store in a cool, dark place for up to 10 years.

BLACKBERRY
Rubus spp.

We have many memories of stained fingers from summer days spent picking berries with our families. Moments like those have inspired our love for blackberries, which deserve a space in every garden. The good news is that there are thornless varieties that are well suited for the edible landscape—cousins to the thorny type found in the wild.

IN THE GARDEN

Blackberry grows reliably in USDA zones 5 to 12, depending on the variety. Unlike vegetables, you plant berries once, and year after year they return, like old friends. The blackberry is a vigorous vine and needs pruning and training to keep it in check, but otherwise it doesn't require much pampering. It prefers full sun and regular water, but it can tolerate some shade; too much shade yields no fruit, however. It thrives in a number of climates and soil conditions but dislikes boggy or nitrogen-depleted soil.

Blackberry canes are somewhat self-supporting but are much easier to handle when grown on a trellis and pruned regularly (see page 207). The fruit grows in tight, compact clusters on second-year stems. This means that you shouldn't prune new growth to the ground if you'd like to have fruit to harvest the following year.

Our favorite thornless blackberries include 'Chester', 'Triple Crown', 'Arapaho', and 'Navaho'. 'Black Butte' and 'Black Satin' are thorny but well worth growing for their beautiful, juicy, delicious fruit.

HARVEST

Don't be concerned if you don't see blackberries the first year. Blackberries produce fruit on second-year floricanes, rather than first-year primocanes. The berries are ready to pick when they are a deep bluish black and plump, and release easily from the branch. Be gentle when harvesting because the berries easily bruise; reduce handling to a minimum and they will keep longer. They are best picked as soon as they are ripe. Store them on your kitchen countertop or in the refrigerator in a berry bowl or small colander for good air circulation and to prevent molding. The berries can be eaten fresh or frozen, or they can be used for jams, jellies, and other sweets. Other juicy, colorful opportunities include blackberry margaritas, infusions, iced tea, ice cream, cobbler, simple syrup, infused water, vinegar, floral arrangements, and, as your fingers will attest, plant dye.

SUMMER PRUNINGS ARRANGEMENT

When your blackberry overwhelms your trellis, grab a vase and create an arrangement. The lovely blooms and fruit (from unripe green to sweet-tasting black) are absolutely charming in a vase.

Because this project involves handling and pruning the plants, make solid, carefully angled cuts on the living stems. Harvest and prune in one snip, at 45- to 60-degree angles. Make the cut slightly above a growth node (bud or branch). You can control the direction of the new shoot growth by cutting above a node that points in the direction you want.

————

Fill a large, crock-style vase with cold, clean water. Wearing gardening gloves, place the cut branches on top of each other on your work surface, forming a bunch. You want a mixture of berry colors, so intersperse the branches with ripe berries among those that are unripe. This arrangement looks best when the blackberry branches cascade over the edge of the vessel, so make sure the branches are long enough to drape. With one hand, grab the whole bunch and cut the ends uniformly. Remove any leaves that might fall below the water line.

15 to 20 blackberry canes of similar lengths, 12 to 36 inches (30 to 90 cm), with berries attached

Place the bunch in a vase all at once, making sure that all the stems are in the water. It should also look very full and lush. If it does not, remove the whole bunch from the vase and add more branches (it is difficult to add or remove branches individually from the vase because they get tangled up in the thorns).

LEMON BEE BALM
Monarda citriodora

_____

Lemon bee balm also bears the nicknames lemon bergamot and wild bergamot because its aroma is similar to that of the bergamot orange, which is used to flavor Earl Grey tea. Medicinally, lemon bee balm has been used to relieve fevers, nausea, headaches, and sore throats. The leaves are used to treat bee stings, which explains the origin of the plant's common name.

IN THE GARDEN

A bona fide bee, butterfly, and hummingbird magnet, lemon bee balm can be grown in USDA zones 3 to 10. Because it is not a reliable perennial in any zone, we consider it an annual. This low-water plant has edible stems and flowers and prefers full sun to part shade. The plants grow from 12 to 30 inches (30 to 75 cm) tall, and their masses of tiered pink-purple flowers bloom from late summer until frost. Plant lemon bee balm where you can best take in its wonderful citrusy scent and easily harvest it for use in the kitchen.

HARVEST

Harvest full stems of flowers and leaves by cutting the stem at the base of the plant. Cut flowers for drying (see page 206) as soon as they're fully open. Use freshly harvested flowers and leaves for garden bouquets and tea. Flowers can be sugared and used to decorate cakes.

LEMON BEE BALM TEA

You might detect hints of Earl Grey in this tea, but rest assured that, unlike the classic tea, this soothing herbal blend won't keep you up at night. The only difference between making tea with dried versus freshly harvested herbs is that you need to steep the latter a bit longer to extract the most flavor.

MAKES 2 CUPS

5 to 7 fresh lemon bee balm stems with both leaves and flowers

1 to 2 slices of dehydrated citrus (see page 206), such as lemon or chinotto orange

2 cups boiling water

Lightly rinse the bee balm stems and flowers in cool water. Remove the bee balm leaves and flowers from the stems. Add the fresh bee balm leaves, flowers, and dried citrus to a teapot. The amount depends on the strength of the herb and how strong you like your tea. Pour the boiling water over the loose tea mix, let steep for about 15 minutes, and then taste. Steep for another 5 minutes if you prefer a stronger tea.

AMARANTH
Amaranthus spp.

The leaves of this heat-loving annual edible taste like spinach, its flowers are perfect for cutting, and its seeds can be used as homegrown grains. Plant it in a cutting garden, in a container, or in the vegetable garden. It adds stunning vertical interest wherever you grow it.

IN THE GARDEN
Native to Asia, amaranth needs space to grow, full sun, warm weather, and consistent moisture. If you live in a humid area, this is the summer plant for you! Plant in succession (see page 207) for a continuous harvest. Plants reach 12 to 24 inches (30 to 60 cm) tall.

Our favorites include the red-leaved varieties such as 'Red Garnet' that feature large, tender leaves with deep red centers; green Callaloo varieties from Jamaica; and love-lies-bleeding (*Amaranthus caudatus*).

HARVEST
Amaranth is very tender and succulent when young, so start harvesting leaves when the plant reaches 10 to 14 inches (25 to 36 cm) tall. As with most summer greens, avoid harvesting during the heat of the day because the greens will wilt quickly and taste bitter. Amaranth leaves will keep in the fridge for up to 2 weeks if wrapped in a cool, damp towel and stored in the crisper. Add young leaves to your salads and add larger leaves to a stir-fry, or you can let your amaranth grow tall and bloom. The flowers are a fun addition to summer bouquets and, if allowed to go to seed, they can be used as a grain or bird food—depending on who gets to the harvest first!

MIDSEASON HERB SALAD

MAKES 4 SERVINGS

4 large handfuls of freshly harvested amaranth leaves

4 to 5 small handfuls of garden herbs, such as anise hyssop leaves, annual basil (large-leaf Italian, purple, 'Genovese', Thai, or globe varieties), dwarf oregano, flat-leaf parsley, nasturtium leaves, rustic arugula, red-stem dandelion or other leaf chicories, tarragon

5 to 10 stems of freshly harvested edible flowers, such as anise hyssop flowers, cilantro flowers, nasturtium flowers, purple basil flowers, rustic arugula flowers

OREGANO VINAIGRETTE

3 tablespoons extra-virgin organic olive oil

1 tablespoon oregano-infused vinegar (see page 66)

Pinch of kosher salt

We love to stroll through the garden with a salad bowl in hand, harvesting and assembling a salad as we go. Don't worry about stems ending up in the bowl, because they can be picked out or chopped up after you've returned to the kitchen.

Amaranth creates an excellent base for this versatile salad because its tender greens complement rather than compete with the strong flavors of the annual herbs (such as parsley, basil, and dwarf oregano). Leafy chicories also mix deliciously with amaranth.

————————

Wash the herbs and flowers in a bowl filled halfway with cold (not warm) water. Gently swish the herbs around to loosen any dirt or lingering insects, lift them out, and place them in salad spinner. Give the herbs a gentle spin, and then lay them on a clean cloth. Tear or chop any large leaves. Keep smaller-leaved herbs such as rustic arugula and globe basil intact.

To make the oregano vinaigrette, in a small bowl, whisk together the olive oil and vinegar, and then add the salt.

Drizzle the salad with the vinaigrette and gently mix. Go lightly with the vinaigrette; too much will result in limp herbs and petals. Serve immediately.

THYME
Thymus spp.

Strolling along a path lined with fragrant thyme is one of the great pleasures of being in the garden. A star member of the mint family and a relative of oregano, this evergreen herb is bountiful in its culinary, medicinal, and ornamental uses.

IN THE GARDEN

Thyme is a hardy perennial in USDA zones 2 to 9. These drought-resistant plants prefer a hot, sunny location with well-drained soil, but they will also tolerate a bit of shade. They grow to a height of 12 to 18 inches (30 to 46 cm) and produce woody stems with small oval leaves.

Thymes bloom in spring and summer, when they attract butterflies and many other beneficial insects and pollinators. Thyme also repels garden pests such as cabbage worms and whiteflies, making it a good companion plant for cabbage, eggplant, potatoes, strawberries, and tomatoes.

Thyme is a staple of the classic vegetable or herb garden and can be used in a multitude of ways. It is often planted between landscape pavers, a look we love, but keep food safety in mind and do not harvest these plants for eating. Do use thyme between stepping stones strictly for ornamental purposes and attracting pollinators, and then plant some extra in an adjacent garden bed where you can harvest it for use in the kitchen.

The most common type is French culinary or English thyme, *Thymus vulgaris*, but we encourage you to grow multiple types. Our favorites include *T. citriodorus* 'Variegated Golden Lemon', various lemon thymes and orange-scented thymes, caraway thyme (*T. herba barona*), and lavender thyme (*T. thracicus*). Each has its own unique flavor.

HARVEST

Pick as needed throughout the growing season. Use the dried leaves (see page 206) during the winter months in the kitchen and the small branches for creating kitchen wreaths and garlands. Thyme blends well with other savory herbs such as French tarragon, rosemary, and savory. It can be used to flavor vinegars, herb butters, teas, poultry, fish, soups, salads, bread, and so much more. Thyme is also wonderful when used to create herbal salves and oils.

CUSTOM HERB BLENDS

BASIC HERB BLEND

MAKES ABOUT ⅓ CUP

3 tablespoons dried
thyme

2 tablespoons dried
dwarf creeping savory

1 tablespoon dried
rosemary

HERBES DE
PROVENCE BLEND

MAKES ABOUT ½ CUP

3 tablespoons dried
thyme

2 tablespoons dried
dwarf creeping savory

1 tablespoon dried
rosemary

1 tablespoon dried
oregano or marjoram

1 tablespoon dried
lavender flowers

CUSTOM GARDEN
BLEND

MAKES ABOUT ½ CUP

3 tablespoons dried
thyme

2 tablespoons dried
dwarf creeping savory

1 tablespoon dried
rosemary

1 to 2 tablespoons dried
anise hyssop flowers,
gem marigolds,
calendula petals, or
other favorites from
your garden

After you've dried your herb harvest, it's time to create your
own custom blend. Herbes de Provence (the classic dried herb
combination of thyme, savory, rosemary, marjoram, and lavender
flowers) provides an excellent foundation for blends, but you can
go even simpler by using only thyme, savory, and rosemary. Start
with this trio, and then work in other favorites from your garden.
Have fun with it.

————

For all the blends, combine the herbs in a shallow bowl, mix by hand,
and transfer to a sealed jar. Store the jar in a cool place (such as a
pantry) out of direct sunlight for up to 6 months.

Use your herb mix to season meats and vegetables before grilling. Add
it to soups, vegetable stews, and egg dishes—really just about anything.

CALAMINTHA
Calamintha nepetoides

_____

Calamintha seems to bloom forever for us, with a flower show that lasts from early summer through the first frost. The frothy flowers complement just about any style of garden.

IN THE GARDEN
Hardy in USDA zones 4 to 9, the perennial calamintha is a close cousin to culinary mint, minus the vigorous spreading habit. This edible and highly fragrant plant grows 12 to 18 inches (30 to 46 cm) tall and twice as wide. An excellent groundcover, it prefers full sun to part shade and can tolerate dry conditions. Kicking off in early summer, a profusion of tiny, tubular flowers in shades of white or pale blue are produced on upright spikes.

The clouds of tiny flowers attract bees, butterflies, and hummingbirds to the garden.

Calamintha is an excellent filler plant in the border garden and makes a beautiful edible edging. Plant it along a path where the leaves' delightful minty scent can be released when you brush against them.

HARVEST
Pinch off flowers and leaves for kitchen use throughout the season, or cut larger stems to add to flower arrangements. Flowers and leaves can keep for a week or longer in a vase away from direct sunlight. We like to help ourselves to these cuttings, often using calamintha throughout the week in our cooking. Leaves can also be dried (see page 206) and are popular in Italian and Middle Eastern cooking. They taste like a combination of mint and oregano. The fragrant foliage is also used to make a minty tea and a soothing lip balm.

HERB & HIVE LIP BALM

It's fun to make your own lip balm from the garden. And if you keep bees, this is also a great way to use your beeswax. Make calamintha-infused olive oil by following the recipe for Calendula-Infused Essential Oil (page 202), substituting calamintha for the calendula.

Place the calamintha olive oil and beeswax into a heatproof glass measuring cup with a pour spout. Fill a saucepan with a couple inches of water. Set the measuring cup into the saucepan and gently warm over medium-low heat until the oil and beeswax melt together. Stir occasionally to ensure that the beeswax melts completely.

MAKES 3 TO 5 TINS

3 tablespoons calamintha-infused olive oil

1 tablespoon beeswax

Carefully remove the measuring cup from the pan. Wipe off the water from the outside of the measuring cup so that no water gets into your lip balm while pouring it into its final containers. Pour the lip balm into containers (such as small tins), and secure the lids. Store in a cool place for up to 3 months.

HUCKLEBERRY
Vaccinium ovatum

We fondly refer to huckleberry as "the blueberry's low-water cousin." Huckleberry has become a go-to shrub for most of the gardens we design because it's got so much going for it: it's a beautiful ornamental with edible fruit and evergreen foliage, and it needs little maintenance.

IN THE GARDEN

Huckleberry is a perennial shrub that is hardy in USDA zones 7 to 9. Although it can thrive on less water after it's established, it happily produces fruit with regular watering and can also tolerate heavy watering. It can be grown in full sun, deep shade, and every light condition in between.

In the sun, plants grow 24 to 36 inches (60 to 90 cm) tall, but shade-grown plants are smaller, at about 10 inches (25 cm). Huckleberry is the perfect shrub to plant under trees, particularly coniferous trees with acidic soil (which it loves). Huckleberry more than compensates for being a slow grower, when in late spring it sends out a show of tiny bell-shaped, pinkish white flowers. New foliage is fabulous, too, starting out bronzy before turning glossy dark green over time.

Huckleberry can easily be grown in containers, but the plants look best when planted in a mass of seven to ten or more, ideally in a woodland landscape. Mass plantings can also be maintained as a natural low hedge. These larger plantings yield a larger harvest, which is great because you'll have enough to share with the birds and wildlife that also love to feast on the sweet berries.

HARVEST

Instead of netting the plants to keep birds and critters out, we opt for planting enough for everyone and harvest often during the fruiting season. We love the small, blackish purple berries, which take time to harvest because of their tiny size—the largest berries are about ½ inch (1.3 cm) wide. Huckleberries are delicate and should be used the day they are picked. The berries provide the fruity basis for jams, pies, and beverages, but they complement savory dishes quite wonderfully as well. Huckleberry stems also hold up beautifully from garden to vase, with dark green oval leaves on green stems that offer an attractive, abundant base for a fresh flower arrangement.

HUCKLEBERRY SHRUB

A shrub is a beverage made from fresh fruit, sugar, and vinegar. Historically, keepers of the kitchen used vinegar as a preservative when refrigeration was not available, hence the development of the shrub, or "drinking vinegar," to preserve the season's fruit harvest.

Thanks to the growing popularity of fermentation in the culinary world, making and drinking shrubs has undergone a revival. We love a good berry shrub (the plant and the drinkable kind) and wanted to share this fun and simple recipe. The vinegar in this crisp and delicious concoction supplies the acidity.

When it's ready to drink, a good rule of thumb is to use 3 tablespoons of shrub to 1 cup of carbonated water in an ice-filled glass. The key is to taste it and adjust accordingly. Finally, garnish with herbs, such as scented geranium or lemon verbena.

MAKES 1½ TO 2 CUPS, ENOUGH FOR ABOUT 10 DRINKS

1 cup fresh huckleberries

1½ cups organic cane sugar

1 cup champagne vinegar

Place the huckleberries in a 1-quart canning jar or fermentation jar (see Resources). In a small saucepan, bring the sugar and vinegar to a brief boil to dissolve the sugar. Pour the hot vinegar mixture over the berries in the jar. Gently macerate, or crush, the huckleberries with a fork to release their flavor.

Seal and store the jar in a cool, dark place for 4 or 5 days. (Note that shrub can be made using the refrigerator in the heat of the summer if cool, dark places are hard to come by. Refrigerator-made shrubs take a little longer to mature, about a month total.) Strain the shrub through a sieve lined with cheesecloth into a clean jar. Cover and chill.

Taste the shrub, and if it's too vinegary, rest assured it will mellow over time. Let it rest for another couple of weeks. Once to your taste, the shrub can be stored in the refrigerator, if it is not there already, for up to 3 months (although they never last that long for us!).

DWARF WINTER SAVORY
Satureja montana 'Nana'

During the transition from summer to fall when many plants start to look weary, this culinary herb puts out a carpet of sweet white flowers that last until first frost. It has a wonderful sprawling habit; let it "creep" through a garden border or cascade from a container. It's charming either way.

'Nana' winter savory is lesser known, with a flavor slightly less spicy than typical winter savory, but it's also an appropriate stand-in for recipes calling for savory. We've found that it dries well, can be easily preserved in salt and dried-herb mixtures, and blends deliciously with many of our other favorite herbs in vinaigrettes.

IN THE GARDEN
Winter savory is a ground-hugging moderate-to low-water plant that prefers well-draining sandy or loamy soils. It thrives in USDA zones 5 to 11, preferring full to partial sun. It is known to deter aphids and other garden pests, making it a good companion plant in the vegetable garden.

Unlike the annual summer savory, winter savory is a hardy perennial edible that dies back in colder climates. It is particularly unfussy in milder climates, and there's no need to cut it back after it goes into winter dormancy because it will leaf out from the stems come spring.

HARVEST
Harvest winter savory fresh as needed, both leaves and stems, until the plant goes dormant. In areas with long growing seasons, cut plants back at the beginning of spring for a second growth and a second harvest. We've learned a wonderful lesson in edible gardening: Many of the plants that are delicious when eaten together also grow well together. Winter savory and pole (vining) beans have long been excellent companions in the garden as well as in the cooking pot. Use this delightful herb fresh, dried (see page 206), or preserved in salt as you would with any recipe calling for standard winter savory. It's great in herb blends, mushroom dishes, potato salads, roasts, cassoulet, stews, and more.

SALT-PRESERVED HERBS

Using salt to preserve herbs is a tried-and-true method that dates back centuries. It's easy to do and wonderfully convenient, because it can be used as the basis for any marinade or salt rub for both meats and grilled vegetables. The fresh herbs permeate every ounce of the salt mixture and release a fragrant, intoxicating aroma that will preserve your garden harvest long after the garden has shifted into winter dormancy.

This recipe can be increased or decreased depending on the size of your harvest.

MAKES 8 OUNCES

15 to 20 stems of garden herbs, including dwarf winter savory, thyme, rosemary, oregano, and parsley

⅔ cup sea salt

Rinse the herbs in cool water and place them on a towel to dry. Destem and coarsely chop the herbs' leaves. Add the salt to the herbs and continue to chop, mixing the two in the process. You want a coarse, not fine, texture. Combine the herbs and salt in a jar, seal the lid securely, and refrigerate. The salt-preserved herbs will last up to a year.

LATE

In late fall, with winter on the horizon, the garden is slowing down with the arrival of cooler nights and shorter days. Seasonal rains can also bring back the deeper, richer colors we associate with this time of year: orange, red, burgundy, and dark green. Harvests include citrus, tubers, and long-awaited fruit such as pineapple and Chilean guava, quince, and persimmon. Herbs can be dried for use during the garden's lean months. Edible flowers and hardier herbs supplement the bounty and can be preserved in the form of infusions and festive garnishes. Our arrangements include branches heavy with fruit and beautiful foliage, and wreaths and bouquets take shape as we head into the holiday season.

QUINCE
Cydonia oblonga

An ancient relative of the apple, quince is easy to grow and adore. The knobby fruit is beautifully imperfect. Come spring, quince flowers infuse the garden with fragrance, and later in the season, the fruit is also wonderfully scented. When planting among other fruit trees, make sure quince is near a path so that you can enjoy its delightful scent.

IN THE GARDEN
Requiring 300 chill hours (see page 207) to produce fruit, quince can be easily grown in USDA zones 5 to 10. Quinces are happy in most soils, as long as they are kept moist throughout the hot days of summer. They do best in full sun but tolerate partial shade. We can't say enough about the sweet scent of those pretty rose-pink blooms, making it a must for the fragrance garden.

·Quince's twisting branches add interest to the winter garden, even when the leaves are gone. In early summer, thin the fruit to about 3 inches (8 cm) apart. If not thinned, the heavy fruit can weigh down the branches, causing them to snap and break.

We think of quince as a well-behaved fruit tree. It stays small, at 12 to 16 feet (3.7 to 5 m), and will not take over your garden. You can plant quince in a pot and keep it in check with summer pruning (see page 207). Favorites include 'Pineapple', 'Smyrna', and 'Van Deman'.

HARVEST
Harvest quince in the fall, when fruits are golden yellow and fragrant. Store them in a cool, dry, dark place on shallow trays, allowing them to mature for about 6 weeks before using. They will keep for up to 3 months. Quince is not eaten fresh but is used as the star ingredient in marmalades, jellies, chutneys, preserves, and paste. It's a lively addition to applesauces and pies and a delicious complement for meat dishes.

QUINCE PASTE

Quince paste, or *membrillo*, is a mainstay in Portuguese and Spanish cuisine. Similar to jelly, it is eaten as dessert, spread on breads and pastries, and used to accompany cheeses. The pulp contains a lot of natural pectin, and as the water boils away in this recipe, the fruit forms a sweet paste. This recipe incorporates the seeds to get the most out of the pectin. When you are cooking quince paste, pay careful attention and stir it frequently to keep it from scorching. Regardless of the texture of the paste, its sweetness is irresistible and welcomes something savory to complement it. Pair it with manchego cheese, or try it with a variety of hard local cheeses.

Peel the quinces, remove the stems, and cut the fruit into 6 to 8 pieces. Core and remove the seeds, and place the seeds in a piece of cheesecloth. Create a pouch with the cloth, tying it closed with cooking twine.

Combine the quince, sugar, water, and seed pouch in a large saucepan. Bring to a boil, lower the heat, and allow it to simmer for 45 minutes, stirring frequently to keep it from sticking to the pot. The quince should deepen in color (some varieties turn a deep amber red). Remove the pan from the heat, let it cool, and remove the seed pouch.

Once cooled, puree the quince using an immersion blender or a food processor until smooth. Spread the paste into an 8 by 8-inch (20 by 20-cm) shallow dish, cover with cellophane or wax paper, and refrigerate for 3 hours. If you prefer a firmer paste, instead of refrigerating, put the dish in a 200°F (94°C) oven for 3 hours to dry out the paste. Then let it cool and refrigerate. The paste keeps for a year in the refrigerator.

MAKES ABOUT 2 CUPS

2 large quinces

1¼ cups organic sugar

1 cup water

ASIAN PERSIMMON

Diospyros kaki 'Fuyu' & 'Hachiya'

Like the magnolia, these persimmons are native to Asia, with large, shiny leaves that are chartreuse in spring and deepen to dark green in summer. But instead of producing showy flowers before new leaf growth in early spring, persimmon treats the eye to brilliant orange leaves in autumn, followed by vibrant orange fruits in winter that ripen after its leaves fall.

IN THE GARDEN

Popular for its ability to produce large fruit on small trees, the deciduous Asian persimmon is hardy in USDA zones 7 to 11 and requires 200 chill hours (see page 207) to fruit. Plant it in full sun for best fruiting and fall color. Persimmon can tolerate most soil types but prefers well-draining, moist, slightly acidic soil. Trees have long taproots. Come planting time, dig the hole a little deeper and loosen the surrounding soil to help the tree establish more quickly. Persimmon can grow 20 to 30 feet (6 to 9 m) tall and wide, so we prune ours annually (see page 207) to maintain a harvestable height. We love 'Fuyu'

and 'Chocolate', which both produce fruits that resemble tomatoes and can be eaten firm or soft. 'Hachiya' is best when it's soft and ripe to the point of falling apart.

HARVEST

'Fuyu' fruits can be picked and eaten right off the tree in November, when the fruit is bright yellow-orange. 'Hachiya' should remain on the tree until it is overripe, or it can be picked hard and ripened indoors. Before eating, 'Hachiya' fruit should be bright orange and feel as soft as jelly; otherwise, you'll get an awful cotton-mouth effect because of the high tannin (an astringent) content. Cut fruit from the branch as close to the fruit as possible. All varieties can be preserved by drying in a dehydrator, and 'Hachiya' pulp stored in the freezer holds up surprisingly (and deliciously) well for a year or more.

'Hachiya' is best for making puddings and breads. 'Fuyu' can be eaten directly from the tree like an apple and is the star of our winter arugula salads. The large, fruit-heavy branches are beautiful to use for wreath making.

PERSIMMON WREATH

If you prune annually to keep your persimmon tree a harvestable height, you can use the prunings for the basis of this beautiful fall wreath. On the delicate side, it will stay fresh for 7 to 14 days and can be placed indoors or out. You will need a 14-inch (36-cm) circular wire wreath frame for this project.

Cut several pieces of hemp twine, or other natural-colored twine, to 10 inches (25 cm) to use to tie the branches around a 14-inch (36-cm) circular wire wreath frame. Place the largest branch onto the top of the frame so that the branch points toward the bottom. The natural curve of the branch should arc around the edge of the frame, and curve slightly inward at the bottom. Attach at the branch to the frame using the twine.

1 freshly cut large persimmon branch (about 3 feet, or 1 m), with fruit and leaves

3 to 4 freshly cut small persimmon branches (1 to 3 feet, or 0.3 to 1 m), with fruit and leaves

After the largest branch is attached, fill in empty spaces with the smaller branches, concentrating all of the branches on the upper half of the frame. This will create an airy, open look. You are not trying to shape the branches into a strict circular wreath; rather, use the natural curve of the branches to form more of a loose oval, with the branches on each side curving in toward each other and hanging down freely at the bottom. Use additional pieces of the twine to secure the branches firmly around the frame. If your wreath is not looking as airy and open as it should, or if the fruits are obscured, trim away some of the small twigs or foliage to achieve more space.

PINEAPPLE GUAVA

Feijoa sellowiana

Pineapple guava boasts a distinctly sweet, aromatic flavor with tropical overtones. Grown as a shrub or small garden tree, this evergreen edible produces an attractive burst of red flowers in the spring followed by mature fruit in the fall. The gorgeous foliage is dark green on the upper surface, silvery gray underneath.

IN THE GARDEN

Pineapple guava is a subtropical perennial plant with considerable cold tolerance, so it will grow well in USDA zones 7 to 11. This highly useful, edible, beautiful shrub's drought tolerance and easygoing nature also make it a great contender for growing in a container—an especially wonderful option if you're growing it in colder regions that would require overwintering the plant indoors (see page 206).

Requiring full sun to partial shade, pineapple guava appreciates afternoon shade in climates with extremely hot summers. It can be grown in full shade but will not fruit regularly. Because of its ability to grow in a variety of light conditions, we use it as a repeating element in our landscape designs. With an upright branching form that can easily be trained as an espalier or small specimen tree, pineapple guava can grow to 15 feet (4.5 m).

We love and appreciate that pineapple guava is considerably unfussy. It seems to grow happily on its own. Once established, it's quite drought tolerant, although it yields better fruit with regular watering. It's also self-pollinating, so only one tree is required to produce fruit.

HARVEST

The blooms of the pineapple guava resemble passionflowers, and they are as pleasing to the palate as they are to the eye. If you harvest only the flower petals, the fruit will continue to grow and ripen in the fall. We think the flowers taste like cotton candy, and you can eat them right off the tree. Or toss them into a salad, add them as a garnish to iced tea or cocktails, or use them for preserves.

The fruit is slightly soft when ripe (similar to a banana). You can test for ripeness by very gently moving the fruit from side to side. If it easily separates from the tree, it's ripe. Ripened fruit also falls freely from the tree and can be harvested from the ground. We eat the fruit by scooping out the pulp and tossing it into a blender to make smoothies, or turning it into a simple syrup for cocktails or sodas. One of the biggest advantages of pineapple guava is that it can be frozen and cooked without loss of flavor from its fragrant, cream-colored flesh. Freeze whole fruit and it will keep for up to a year.

PINEAPPLE GUAVA SIMPLE SYRUP

Simple syrup is a staple for cocktail makers. This version is a simple infusion of fruit, water, and sugar, liquefied to flavor carbonated water and cocktails. Crafting a simple syrup is a fantastic way to extract the essence of the fruit without having to use the pulp and seeds. The sweet, tropical nature of pineapple guava makes it the perfect addition for cocktails, homemade sodas, and smoothies.

For a tropical homemade soda, mix 1 tablespoon (or more to taste) pineapple guava simple syrup into 8 ounces carbonated water. Or, use to make a refreshing and regenerating pineapple guava and kale smoothie (pictured opposite) by placing 1 apple (peeled and cored), ¼ cup pineapple guava simple syrup (or 2 fresh pineapple guavas, peeled), 1 banana, 6 kale leaves, 1 cup unsweetened almond milk, and 4 ice cubes in your blender and blend completely until smooth. Pour into a glass and enjoy.

––––––––––

MAKES ABOUT 3 CUPS

2 cups pineapple guava pulp, roughly chopped, from 15 to 20 fruit (depending on size)

2 cups organic sugar

2 cups water

2 teaspoons lemon juice

Place the pineapple guava pulp in a nonreactive saucepan and gently bring it to a boil, stirring frequently to prevent sticking. Once the fruit breaks down (about 10 minutes), remove the pan from the heat, let the mixture cool slightly, and then pour it through a sieve into a bowl. Press the pulp with a wooden spoon to maximize the amount of juice extracted. Discard the seeds and larger bits of fruit in the sieve.

Combine the strained pulp with the sugar, water, and lemon juice in a clean nonreactive pan. Place it over medium-high heat and bring to a simmer, stirring to prevent sticking. Once the sugar has dissolved (about 5 minutes), remove the mixture from the heat and let it cool slightly.

Use a funnel to pour the hot liquid into a clean jar or bottle and seal with a lid. Let it cool, and then store it in the refrigerator. It will keep for up to a year.

'BERGGARTEN' SAGE

Salvia officinalis 'Berggarten'

The dried leaves of *Salvia officinalis* 'Berggarten', or tea sage, can be added to tea or herb blends. In the garden, 'Berggarten' sage has a clean, mounding habit, requires next to no maintenance, and emits a classic earthy aroma. It may not be a reliable bloomer in some zones, but that's OK, because it's all about the leaves—plump and oval shaped, their soft gray-greenness makes you want to reach out and touch them.

IN THE GARDEN

Available in green and variegated forms, 'Berggarten' sage thrives in full sun as a perennial plant in USDA zones 5 to 8, where the stunning purple edible flowers pop in June or July. In all other hardiness zones, it can be grown as an annual or can be overwintered indoors (see page 206). It is compact, woody stemmed, and shrubby in nature, typically growing 12 to 24 inches (30 to 60 cm) tall. The strongly aromatic gray-green leaves can measure 4 inches (10 cm) across, substantially longer than many garden-variety sages.

Drought tolerant and deer resistant, 'Berggarten' sage is a garden standout in so many ways. We love how its fuzzy, floppy leaves mix with other perennials in a container, border, or rock garden. It also looks great cascading over a raised bed in herb or vegetable plots.

Prune back as necessary for shaping in early in spring or fall. Don't prune into old woody growth, because this may stress the plant. If the base of the plant becomes woody, replace the plant.

HARVEST

Harvest fresh leaves as needed throughout the growing season, and harvest larger stems for preserving before the first frost. Dried sage (see page 206) has a stronger flavor than fresh sage, and we like to have it on hand throughout the winter for use in the kitchen. We use it like common culinary sage. It makes a fun pesto and a soothing tea. Flash-fry the leaves and sprinkle them on fresh pasta or soup. Add stems to cut-flower arrangements, kitchen wreaths, and garlands.

SAGE GARLAND

During the late season before the first frost, we harvest stems of 'Berggarten' sage for drying purposes. This beautiful garland first adorns the center of our dining table and is later hung to complete the drying process. This garland will fit nicely on a 6-foot (1.8-m) table. You will need 3 to 5 yards of 28-gauge floral paddle wire for this project, depending upon the size of your garland.

————

Lay a stem of sage on top of one end of a 7-foot (2-m) length of hemp twine or other natural-colored twine, with the sage leaves hiding the end of the twine and the stem·end pointing down the length of twine. The twine will be the structure upon which the garland is built. Wrap 28-gauge paddle wire (the kind florists use), still attached to the spool, three or four times around the stems and the piece of twine.

Keeping the wire attached to the spool, lay the second stem of sage just below the top of the wrapped first stem, slightly overlapping so that the leaves of the second piece cover the stem of the first piece, and wrap the wire around both stems and the twine. Continue adding sage and wrapping wire down the length of the twine.

When the garland has reached the desired length, turn the last stem of sage backward and tuck it into the end; then wrap it with wire to secure it in place.

25 to 30 fresh 'Berggarten' sage stems with leaves (make harvesting cuts as long as possible, and use fewer stems for a smaller table)

Place the finished garland on your table and enjoy it as a beautifully scented fall decoration for up to 2 days. After that, you can hang the garland in a cool, dry place to finish drying, which will take about 10 days to dry completely. Use sage leaves directly from the garland as needed, or remove all of the leaves at once and store them in a jar. The dried sage will last for up to a year in your pantry.

SHUNGIKU
Glebionis coronaria

A member of the daisy family and native to the Mediterranean region, shungiku is known as the edible chrysanthemum. Although all chrysanthemum flower petals are technically edible, their taste differs widely from plant to plant. We love this one in particular, not only because it's bursting with flavor, but it's an easy-to-grow cool-season annual with beautiful leaves that resemble the foliage of its ornamental cousins. Both the leaves and stems of shungiku are harvested for use either fresh in salads or cooked in soups, stews, and stir-fries. Better still, the dark green, aromatic leaves are rich in minerals and vitamin B. The white-and-yellow flowers are also flavorful—a claim not all chrysanthemums can make.

IN THE GARDEN
Shungiku is an annual in USDA zones 8 to 12 and easy to grow from seed. Sow successively in spring and throughout the summer. Late-sown plants are hardy and will provide a winter harvest. Plants appreciate light shade in the heat of summer and full sun in the cooler fall and winter months. Shungiku prefers fertile, well-drained, moist soil and cooler temperatures. Plants reach 12 to 18 inches (30 to 46 cm) tall. They make a beautiful addition to kitchen gardens, cut-flower gardens, containers, and window boxes.

HARVEST
Harvest leaves and young stems when the plant is 4 to 6 inches (10 to 15 cm) tall, being careful to leave the flower buds so that you can harvest the edible flowers when they bloom as well. The herbs and flowers can keep for approximately 2 weeks in the refrigerator if you gently rinse in a bowl of cold water, lightly spin dry in salad spinner, place on a dry cloth, and put in the crisper drawer. Use the flower petals as a garnish for soups and salads. Young leaves can be cooked like spinach or used in fresh salads. Lightly steamed or boiled, these greens have a mildly grassy, herbaceous taste. Open flowers and unopened flower buds (pearls) can be used to make a beneficial herbal tea. The Japanese dip the flowers in sake and eat them at the beginning of a meal to confer good health and long life.

LATE-SEASON HERB SALAD

MAKES 4 SERVINGS

4 large handfuls of freshly harvested winter herbs and greens including shungiku leaves, chervil, baby Swiss chard, fine-leaf mustard greens such as 'Ruby Streaks', purple or green choi, celery or lovage leaves, flat-leaf parsley, chives or green tops of overwintering onions, salad burnet, pink purslane, nasturtium leaves, sorrel, and marjoram

5 to 10 stems of edible flowers, such as shungiku blooms, violas, calendula petals, mustard or kale flowers, borage, and mashua

Simple Champagne Vinaigrette (see page 30)

Kosher or sea salt

This recipe makes use of the last of the growing season's green bounty. If you live in a colder climate, this could be the last of your herb salads. In our neck of the woods, we prepare this salad even when temperatures drop. Shungiku's wonderful minty taste is a perfect companion to sturdy cool-season Asian greens, chards, and mustards.

———————

Rinse herbs and edible flowers in a bowl half-filled with cold (not warm) water. Gently swish the herbs and flowers to loosen any dirt or lingering insects. Place in salad spinner for a gentle spin, and then lay the herbs on a dry cloth. The herbs must sufficiently dry so that the vinaigrette will adhere to them.

Tear or chop large leaves and thinly slice leafy herbs that are bold flavored, such as sorrel, fine-leafed mustards, and celery or lovage leaves. Add the herbs and leaves to a large salad bowl. Drizzle with vinaigrette, sprinkle with salt, and gently toss the salad. Just before serving, remove the petals from the edible flowers (avoiding the bitter centers) and use them as a garnish atop the salad.

AUSTRALIAN FINGER LIME
Microcitrus australasica

A favorite among chefs, this special citrus is well worth seeking out. The petite, elongated fruits are the shape and size of your finger, and they are bursting with a flavor reminiscent of true limes. "Citrus caviar" is a fitting nickname because of the fruit's caviar-like bubbles of tangy flesh that pop on your tongue.

IN THE GARDEN

Native to Australia, finger lime is a perennial evergreen in USDA zone 10. It can be grown elsewhere, but it must be overwintered indoors (see page 206) in colder areas. In colder climates, grow it in a container for easy transition indoors as the temperatures drop. Finger lime does not go dormant in the winter, and because it needs 8 to 12 hours of sunlight each day, place the plant in a sunny window. It can, however, tolerate less sun and will grow in partial shade.

Unlike other citrus, finger lime has small myrtle-shaped leaves and flowers that look great in containers. You can also plant several finger limes in the landscape to create an edible hedgerow. Place them in the center of the garden bed, away from paths, however, because this beauty has big thorns.

Don't be fooled by its delicate appearance. This plant is tough in the landscape—the only citrus in our gardens that can thrive in a lower water setting. Like all citrus, it prefers well-drained soil. It is, however, a bit less finicky than other citrus and doesn't need as much fertilizer. We rarely give it much more than a topping of good organic compost at the base of the plant when it stops fruiting, followed by an annual application of organic citrus fertilizer after it has flowered and set new fruit.

HARVEST

Begin your finger lime harvest after fruit has reached finger length, or about 4½ inches (12 cm) long. Harvest can occur year-round, with peak harvest lasting from late November to January. High in vitamin C, finger lime elevates the flavor and texture profile of many foods and beverages. You can eat it immediately after it ripens or store it in the refrigerator for 3 to 4 weeks.

To use, cut the fruit in half lengthwise and push your finger into the skin to release the tart flesh. Or make a slit at the top of the fruit and push your thumbs up from the bottom of the fruit, forcing the caviar through the slit. The translucent, greenish white or pinkish vesicles in the inner flesh of the finger lime are filled with juice. Round and firm, they pop like caviar as you bite them. We use the caviar instead of lime or lemon juice with fish tacos, raw oysters, and fresh salmon, but our favorite way to use it is in gin and tonics.

PAPA'S FINGER LIME GIN & TONIC

MAKES 1 DRINK

1 cup ice

2 ounces St. George
Botanivore gin

5 ounces Fever Tree
tonic

1 lime

2 finger limes

Regardless of how you extract the citrus caviar, finger lime
brings a refreshing level of excitement to the kitchen. This recipe
was handed down to us from Alethea's stepfather, Papa. Enjoy!

————

Fill a 12-ounce mason jar with the ice, gin, and tonic. Cut the lime in
half and squeeze the juice into the jar. Cut the finger limes in half
lengthwise, and use your finger to push the citrus caviar into the jar.
Let it rest on top of the ice cubes as a garnish.

CHILEAN GUAVA
Ugni molinae

_____

You're not likely to find this rare fruit in supermarkets. The lovely, evergreen Chilean guava is as prized for its shiny, scented foliage as it is for its late-season aromatic berries. The glossy, evergreen foliage is dense like boxwood, which hints at its membership in the myrtle family. New growth is a bronze-burgundy color. In spring, fragrant, tiny, white bell-shaped flowers cover the shrub. Its deep red, blueberry-size fruits smell wonderful and are packed with a surprising amount of flavor considering their diminutive size. A true winter treat.

IN THE GARDEN
Chilean guava is an excellent foundation shrub, and its new growth is particularly attractive against a backdrop of neutral tones. Use it in place of boxwood as an edible hedge or to define a potager or kitchen garden.

This exciting, decidedly underused perennial shrub is hardy in USDA zones 7 to 10 but can be overwintered indoors (see page 206) in colder areas. It grows 5 to 6 feet (1.5 to 1.8 m) tall and wide, and, because of its slower nature, it makes an easy shrub to prune as needed (see page 207) to keep it in a tidy shape. Chilean guava is so low maintenance that a gentle clipping now and then is all it really needs. It can live in sun to part shade, in dry or moist soil, and it can tolerate drought. Plus it's self-pollinating and pest-free. 'Flambeau', a highly ornamental Chilean guava with variegated leaves, is equally delicious and slightly hardier than the nonvariegated type.

HARVEST
Astoundingly aromatic and fabulously flavorful, the berries are a real late-season treat, ripening slowly, usually in early winter. When ripe, berries are fragrant with a bit of a give when squeezed. The best way to determine if they are ripe is to try one. If the berry is sweet, has a soft center like a blueberry, and is fragrant, then it is ripe. The leaves can be harvested throughout the year. The berries and leaves should be used the day they are picked. The berries are similar in taste to wild strawberry and make a tasty jam. You can also soak them in gin and sugar to produce a Chilean version of sloe gin. The leaves can be used for tea, and word has it that roasted Chilean guava seeds can be used as a coffee substitute. In addition, winter prunings make a beautiful homegrown arrangement.

PETITE UGNI ARRANGEMENT

Late-season prunings are the basis for this sweet arrangement that can be assembled in minutes.

3 branches of
variegated Chilean
guava, 8 to 18 inches
(20 to 46 cm) long

1 stem of flowering
camellia, 8 inches
(20 cm) long, or other
winter-blooming
flower

2 to 3 branches of
Chilean guava, 8 to
18 inches (20 to 46 cm)
long, plus a couple of
smaller sprigs

1 piece of camellia
foliage, 8 inches
(20 cm) long

_____

In a vase with a small opening no more than 2 inches (5 cm) in diameter, add the branches of variegated Chilean guava, concentrating the placement in the center of the vase so that the fruit is visible. Add the camellia flower toward the front of the arrangement to balance the fruit and create a focal point.

Add 1 or 2 longer pieces of the Chilean guava to the right and left sides of the arrangement, letting them arch over the sides of the vase. Tuck a couple of smaller sprigs of Chilean guava in the center to break up the variegated guava. Finish by adding the camellia foliage to the back of the arrangement, its large leaves providing a backdrop to the smaller guava leaves in front.

CHINOTTO ORANGE
Citrus myrtifolia

Also known as the myrtle-leaf orange, chinotto is a variety of sour orange that produces some of the most abundant, fragrant blossoms of all citrus species. It is also more cold hardy than the average sweet orange. The chinotto fruit is a key ingredient in *amaro* (Italian bitters), bitter orange Italian sodas, and the Italian apéritif, Campari.

IN THE GARDEN
Hardy in USDA zones 8 to 10, chinotto can be grown in all zones if plants are grown in containers and brought indoors in winter (see page 206). It requires abundant sunlight and moist, well-drained soil. Reaching only 3 to 5 feet (1 to 1.5 m) tall, this small but highly decorative perennial shrub has dense, glossy foliage that resembles boxwood or myrtle. It's a perfect container tree and is sometimes used for bonsai.

To grow chinotto in colder climates, keep it in a container for easy transition indoors over the winter. Citrus requires 8 to 12 hours of sunlight each day and does not go dormant in the winter—that is, it retains its leaves. If you bring your chinotto indoors, place it in a sunny window.

HARVEST
The tart fruit grows in clusters, ripening in November to March, and can cling to the tree for most of the year—hence its highly prized ornamental appeal. Fruits turn yellow when they are ripe, and you can leave ripe fruit hanging on the tree for up to a year until you want to use it. Sour oranges are typically not eaten fresh. Their culinary importance lies in the oil extracted from the flowers, leaves, seeds, rind, and flesh, making them ideal for infusions. The fruits can also be candied and used in marmalade. The dried flowers and buds (see page 206) can be used in tea blends.

VIN D'ORANGE

This project is a test of patience but yields a huge reward. *Vin d'orange*, a traditional wine/alcohol infusion made with bitter oranges, just gets better with age—even years. We cannot always wait that long and usually break into it by summer when we pour it over ice for an amazingly refreshing beverage on a balmy night; garnish with an orange wedge, or serve it straight up as an aperitif. *Vin d'orange* can also be used in cocktails instead of Lillet or sweet vermouth. Traditionally made with Seville oranges, we use chinotto, and although any white wine or rosé can be used, we prefer to keep it French and use a nice Sancerre.

———

**MAKES ABOUT
1½ QUARTS**

1 cup organic sugar

1 cup vodka

15 chinotto oranges

1 vanilla bean pod, sliced in half

2 to 3 whole star anise pods

2 (750-ml) bottles Sancerre wine

Pour the sugar and vodka into a 2-quart jug. Stir with a wooden spoon until the sugar is dissolved. Slice the oranges and add to the jar, including the seeds, stirring again. Add the vanilla bean, star anise, and Sancerre wine. Cover the infusion with a lid and store in a cool, dark place.

Stir the mixture occasionally, but otherwise let it sit for 30 days. Then taste to check the flavor. It should taste like orange with a slight bitter tang. If you prefer a stronger bite, continue to infuse for 10 days more.

Strain the *vin d'orange* through a strainer lined with a few layers of cheesecloth. For a clearer infusion, strain it again. Decant the strained *vin d'orange* into bottles or jars. Store it in the refrigerator. It will keep longer than you can resist drinking it.

TURMERIC
Curcuma longa

Designated a true superfood because of its anti-inflammatory and antioxidant qualities, turmeric is perfect for the colder season when we should all be boosting our immune systems. Commonly referred to as queen lily or Indian saffron, turmeric is a tropical plant from the ginger family. It boasts large, attractive leaves and gorgeous white flowers, which give the garden a lush, tropical look. The leaves and stems are edible, but it's really all about the beautiful knobby rhizomes, or knobby roots, from which the colorful, flavorful spice is created.

IN THE GARDEN
Turmeric is a perennial herb in USDA zones 7 to 10, where the rhizomes can be left in the ground to go dormant in winter and sprout new flowers in the spring. In colder climates, dig up the rhizomes after the plant dies back from frost. Save some to eat and some to overwinter indoors (see page 206) to plant again in the spring.

Turmeric thrives best in full to partial sun, but it can also grow up to 4 feet (1.2 m) tall in light shade. Note that prolonged growing in heavy shade will reduce the size of the rhizome harvest. As with most other tropical plants, turmeric needs to be watered regularly.

Turmeric cannot be planted by seed; instead, start turmeric plants by planting its rhizomes (see Resources). It produces tall, exceptionally beautiful white flower spikes. The flower is so attractive that it is worth growing turmeric for this alone.

HARVEST
Although the leaves and stems are edible, most people harvest turmeric for its rhizomes, which are harvested 9 to 10 months after planting. You will know when they are ready because the plant's leaves will turn yellow and begin to die back. Gently dig up half of the rhizomes for use and leave the other half for the next year's garden. Once harvested, store the rhizomes in a cool, dark place, as you would with dahlia rhizomes. They last about as long as fresh ginger in the refrigerator (about 2 weeks), but they can be frozen for several months for later use.

The harvested rhizomes can be used fresh as well. Remove the outer skin, wearing gloves, because the rhizome can stain your fingers yellow, which makes it an excellent plant dye. Use it to make essential oils, tinctures, and tea, and preserve turmeric by drying the tubers (see Turmeric Powder, page 174). Small leaves can be added to salads, or use larger leaves to wrap around fish to flavor it during cooking.

TURMERIC DYE

To preserve your harvest, you can make a turmeric powder to be used in cooking and as a luscious plant dye. Turmeric makes the happiest sunshine-yellow dye with a deep, saturated hue that lasts through hundreds of washings. In this recipe, we'll use a cotton muslin table runner. It looks beautiful on the table with a collection of mismatched ceramics and handmade wooden plates.

To achieve interesting dye patterns, bunch the fabric tightly into a ball before dunking it in the dye bath. Everything will be exposed to the dye except the areas that are in the innermost parts of the bundled fabric; these parts will be much lighter depending on the tightness of bundle. For more dyeing basics, see page 206.

———————

To make the turmeric powder, place the turmeric rhizomes in a nonreactive saucepan, cover with water, and boil for 45 minutes. Drain the rhizomes, let them cool enough to handle, and then peel. Place the peeled turmeric on a cooling rack and let it dry for about a week. Then use a coffee grinder or food processor to grind the dried turmeric into a fine yellow powder. Store the powder in a closed container indefinitely.

TURMERIC POWDER
4 turmeric rhizomes

To prepare the fabric to accept the dye, mix the salt and water in a large stockpot and set over medium heat. Add the table runners and allow to simmer for 30 minutes. Remove the fabric, let cool to the touch, and wring it out. You'll be adding the wet fabric to the dye, so set aside.

FABRIC AND FIXATIVE
½ cup table salt

8 cups water

1 or 2 white
100% cotton muslin
table runners

To prepare the dye, in a medium saucepan, combine the turmeric powder and water and bring to a boil.

TURMERIC DYE
¼ cup turmeric
powder (above)

4 cups water

Add the wet fabric to the dye and simmer for 30 minutes to achieve a softer color, or for about an hour if you want a darker color. Remember that wet fabric always looks darker until it is rinsed and wrung out. Remove the fabric from the dye bath, rinse it with cold water until the water runs clear, wring it out, and hang to dry. Remember that the dye will drip from the fabric as it dries, so hang it in an appropriate place to avoid staining.

VIOLA

Viola odorata & V. tricolor

Long ago, viola was believed to have healing properties that provided comfort to those suffering from heartache. The *Viola* genus comprises a large group of cheerful, edible flowering plants. The most well known are *Viola odorata* (sweet violet) and *V. tricolor* (Johnny-jump-up or wild pansy).

The petals of sweet violet vary from deep violet to white and are quite fragrant. We have a particular soft spot for the deep purple 'Queen Charlotte'. Sweet violet's sister, *V. tricolor*, typically bears a brilliant purple and yellow flower with a white face, a vibrant color trio that, among numerous other virtues, makes it a must for every home garden.

IN THE GARDEN

Depending on the variety, violas can be grown as an annual, biennial, or perennial in USDA zones 2 to 9. Conventionally used as bedding annuals due to their small stature (6 inches, or 15 cm), viola will self-seed each year. They benefit from a light trimming in early summer to encourage new growth for a second fall display. They will flower throughout the winter in climates with mild weather.

In regions with cool summers, viola thrives in full sun, and in warmer climates it does best in part to light shade. Both deer and rabbit resistant, the plants prefer regular water during summer but can tolerate dry shade. The tiny blooms make a sweet cut flower, plus they're edible fresh or candied.

HARVEST

Harvest single flowers for garnishes and infusions, or full stems for salads and the vase. The foliage and flowers of viola are as nutritious as they are pretty. The leaves contain healthful vitamins and minerals, and the blooms are rich in vitamin C. (Avoid eating the roots and seeds because they can be irritating to some.) The flowers make a beautiful, edible garnish for salads or atop cakes, and can be blended into compound butters and sprinkled on soft cheeses. Use viola leaves in place of or in addition to other green leafy vegetables by adding them to salads, soups, and steamed or sautéed greens. You can also use the leaves to make tea or an olive oil or water infusion.

EDIBLE FLOWER-INFUSED WATER

The calming qualities of this vitamin C–packed infusion make it a wonderful treat in the winter and early spring months. It's a delicious and refreshing way to savor your viola harvest.

MAKES 2 CUPS

35 to 40 viola flowers, plus extra for garnish

2 cups cool water

Ice cubes

½ cup lemon juice (optional)

Place the viola flowers in a jar or pitcher, and cover with the cool water. After 30 minutes, pour the viola water over ice and garnish with some of the edible blooms, or add lemon juice for a refreshing viola lemonade.

BORAGE
Borago officinalis

In a shade of blue rarely seen in the world of edible flowers, bright and cheery borage blossoms taste like cucumber, which makes it easy to see why borage has traditionally been used in salads and lemonade. This annual is a bee and butterfly magnet in a cutting garden, vegetable patch, or container.

IN THE GARDEN

Borage is more than just a pretty herb. It can be your edible garden's guardian and best friend. Strawberries tend to fruit more heavily in its presence. It keeps hornworms off the tomatoes and increases yields of cucumbers, gourds, and many fruiting plants. Other plants that seem to improve when grown near borage include beans, grapes, squash, and peas.

Easy-to-grow borage is a hardy, cool-season annual that thrives in the late and early seasons, boasts a long harvest period, and can be grown all year long in mild climates. It's not particular about soil but appreciates regular watering. A fast grower, it usually reaches 18 to 35 inches (46 to 90 cm) tall and bears hundreds of flower clusters. It also self-sows readily. Planting in full sun will help plants grow sturdier. Borage is also disease, deer, and pest resistant and can tolerate heat and humidity.

HARVEST

Harvest stems and place them immediately in cool water. The colorful blooms will brighten your kitchen counter as they wait to be used. Salads, cold drinks, desserts, and even ice cubes become more beautiful and delicious with the addition of borage. You can also make a simple syrup that includes the leaves and flowers to add a kick of cucumber flavor to drinks. The petals of the blue, star-shaped flowers keep their color when added to liquids and even when frozen.

EDIBLE FLOWER GARNISH

Adding edible flowers to your cooking and cocktails is a surprisingly easy way to use your harvest. They add fresh dabs of color and introduce unique flavors to your dishes.

As always, use only edible flowers that have been grown organically and not sprayed with chemicals or pesticides. Pick the flowers in the coolest part of the day, usually the morning. Most edible flowers have bitter centers, so we usually eat only the petals. For borage, we also remove the thorny backside of the flower. Once you've finished garnishing your dish or beverage, you can save leftover petals by wrapping them in a cloth and storing them in the crisper of your refrigerator for up to 2 weeks.

Here are a few of our tried-and-true favorites.

- Anise hyssop: Add to summer fruit salads and iced teas
- Bachelor's buttons: Garnish cakes and cupcakes
- Borage: Garnish Champagne, Pimm's Cups, and other cocktails
- Calamintha: Garnish vegetable salads, pasta dishes, roasted vegetables, and mushroom bruschetta
- Calendula: Garnish salads, sushi, fresh spring rolls, desserts, and avocado toast
- Flowering basils: Garnish tomato salads, herbal iced tea, and summer cocktails
- Gem marigolds: Float them in cocktails, especially Gin and Tonics
- Lilac: Garnish vanilla cupcakes or scones, add to lemon-based beverages and salads
- Mashua: Garnish salads and Bloody Marys
- Peppermint candy flower: Garnish cheeses, salads, and desserts
- Rose: Add to salads, use to top ice cream and baked desserts, float in summer punch bowls
- Viola: Garnish salads, iced scones, shrubs, and desserts

BAY LAUREL

Laurus nobilis

If you've purchased bay leaf, you know that a small jar can be costly. Planting your own bay laurel tree will not only provide free leaves to flavor your favorite dishes, but it will also embellish your garden with its lush evergreen foliage and refreshing herbal scent for years to come.

IN THE GARDEN

Bay laurel can be reliably grown as a perennial in USDA zones 8 to 11, and potted laurel can be overwintered indoors in colder climates. Requiring low water once established, this sun-loving Mediterranean garden staple offers an aesthetically pleasing structure in addition to its culinary uses. The dark green foliage is valued as a flavorful seasoning, but the tree can also spice up your garden. It thrives in containers, which is ideal if space is a concern or if you need to move it indoors for the winter (see page 206).

We keep our bay laurel trimmed to 8 feet (2.4 m) tall for easy harvest. Bay laurel requires little maintenance other than pruning (see page 207), which not only keeps the tree from getting too big (trees can reach 60 feet, or 18 m, tall), but provides a steady supply of leafy bundles for drying in the kitchen and for sharing.

HARVEST

Harvest branches throughout the year as you prune your trees to keep them at a desired height. Dried leaves have a shelf life of 1 to 3 years if stored in a sealed container. The pungent flavor explains their popularity for use in countless dishes and as a primary ingredient in the *bouquet garni*, an herb bundle traditionally used to prepare soup. Even when a recipe doesn't call for bay leaf, we find ourselves slipping in a leaf or two. Remember to remove the leaves from the soup before serving! Although the fresh leaves can be used in cooking, we prefer the convenience and taste of dried bay laurel (see page 206), which are richer in flavor than fresh leaves. (If you are using fresh leaves, double the amount of bay leaf your recipe calls for because they are not as strong as dried leaves.) Bay leaves can also be used in a kitchen wreath.

BAY LAUREL KITCHEN WREATH

When you grow your own bay laurel, you will have plenty on hand to make wreaths for drying and decoration. This modern interpretation of a wreath goes beyond the traditional circular shape, enabling the branches to flow more gracefully. Hang it in your kitchen and snap off dried bay leaves for cooking as needed. The beautiful and pliable fresh stems of the bay make it a cinch to create. Make sure to prune your tree as you harvest (see page 207) and make your cut at a growth point on the bay laurel stem. You will need a 14-inch (36-cm) circular wire wreath frame for this project.

3 long fresh bay laurel branches, 24 to 48 inches (60 to 120 cm)

2 to 3 short fresh bay laurel branches, 12 to 24 inches (30 to 60 cm)

Using twine, attach the longest, straightest bay laurel branch horizontally to the center left side of a 14-inch (36-cm) circular wire wreath frame, so that it horizontally bisects the frame. Tie the other smaller branches to the left side of the frame as well, so that they point in the same direction but arc above or below the central branch. Secure all the branches on the frame using extra pieces of twine.

Hang the wreath in your kitchen or pantry. The leaves will be dry in 3 to 5 days. Use leaves from the wreath as needed or enjoy the wreath over a mantle or on the wall. When you are ready for a change, remove the leaves from the wreath and store them in a sealed jar for later to use in all your signature dishes. Dried leaves will keep for up to 3 years.

ROSEMARY
Rosmarinus officinalis

Aromatic and evergreen, rosemary is a staple in our gardens. It's as useful and beautiful as it is edible, which would explain why it inspires us to use it often for hedging and structure. From late winter through early spring, the plant displays blue flowers that brighten the garden. Popular with pollinators, rosemary provides needed winter blooms to keep bees happy during the colder times of the year.

IN THE GARDEN
Rosemary is a perennial grower in USDA zones 6 to 10. Where winter hardy, it can be grown in herb gardens, along borders, or as foundation plantings. Rosemary can take on a variety of roles in the garden, from ornamental specimen plant to low hedge. Container plantings bring its beautiful fragrance to patios, decks, and any other sunny areas. In areas with colder winters, grow it in pots and overwinter it indoors (see page 206).

Rosemary needs well-drained soil and full sun, but it will tolerate light shade. Established plants are drought tolerant. Other than some light winter pruning for shape and height control, they are relatively easy to care for, as long as you don't overwater them.

The many varieties of available rosemary include those with upright, creeping, and dwarf forms, and those that feature white or blue flowers. For hedging and to provide structure in the landscape, we often turn to 'Tuscan Blue', which typically grows 4 to 6 feet (1.2 to 1.8 m) tall in winter-hardy areas. For rock or herb gardens, or to provide an evergreen garden edging, we love the more compact 'Chef's Choice' because of its smaller size (12 to 18 inches, or 30 to 46 cm) and cascading growth.

HARVEST
Harvest year-round as needed, using garden clippers to make clean pruning cuts. Place cut sprigs directly in cool water for fresh use or dry them to use later (see page 206). Rosemary has multiple uses outside and inside the home. Its leaves (fresh or dried) are delightful as an herbal flavoring in cooking, herbal butters, and vinegar infusions.

Drop a rosemary sprig into bath water, add several to a bouquet or wreath, or wrap it around a napkin ring at the table. Burn a bundle of rosemary branches over charcoal when grilling to enhance the flavor of meats, or use a sprig as an edible skewer.

SMUDGE STICKS

Sprigs of rosemary become the makings of our own garden smudge sticks, used traditionally to bring about mental clarity and calmness and to release negative energy. Smudge sticks are dried herb bundles that are burnt as incense, releasing a rustic aroma that's relaxing and pleasant. Red string is traditionally used to tie the bundles in ceremonies in many cultures, but we take our cue from rosemary herself and use electric blues to match her winter blooms.

————

Divide the rosemary branches into three groups of four branches. It's easier to bundle the smudge stick if the stems are the same length, so group similarly sized cuttings together. Cut some cotton thread into three pieces, each approximately 6 feet (1.8 m) long. Double each piece by folding it in half.

Leaving a 6-inch (15-cm) tail of thread, start wrapping the rosemary bundle continuously (at least ten times) in one place, about 1 inch (2.5 cm) above the bottom of the stems. Make a knot to secure the band of thread and keep it in place. Wrap the bundle tightly, spiraling up toward the top of the stems. Fold in any stray sprigs, tucking them under the thread as you go. Once you reach the top of the bundle, continue wrapping, crisscrossing the string as you head back down toward the base. Tie the loose end to the original knot at the base of the bundle.

MAKES 3 SMUDGE STICKS

12 rosemary branches, each 6 to 12 inches (15 to 30 cm) long

Let your fresh smudge sticks dry flat for 1 to 3 weeks. When they are dry and ready, light one end (blowing out the flame itself) to release its smoky scent while holding on to the other end.

POMEGRANATE
Punica granatum

Pomegranate, long considered a symbol of fertility, has been grown and eaten for millennia. Its reputation must be a result of its abundance of appealing qualities. The tree produces fruit that provides beautiful spots of bright red in the landscape. In fall, its foliage changes to a gorgeous hot yellow. The fruit is beloved for its tangy flavor and exceptional antioxidant properties. We honor the pomegranate for all these reasons, plus it's just that perfect bridge plant as fall transitions into winter.

IN THE GARDEN

Pomegranate originates from the Middle East. Most pomegranates are hardy in USDA zones 7 to 10 and prefer well-drained soils. They grow best in full sun, although the shrubs will tolerate some shade. Most varieties are self-pollinating and require only 150 chill hours (see page 207) to produce fruit.

Pomegranate can be grown as a multiple-trunk shrub or as a standard tree that grows 15 to 25 feet (4.5 to 7.5 m) tall. It can also be espaliered, or trained to grow flat against a wall. In a small space or near a pathway, plant pomegranate as a standard tree, because the shrubs can spread spiny branches into walkways, poking passersby. Keep your pomegranate pruned at 6 to 8 feet (1.8 to 2.4 m) tall for easy harvest. Unfussy and easy to maintain, pomegranate should be pruned during the winter (see page 207). Our favorites include 'Wonderful', 'Ambrosia', and 'Eversweet'.

HARVEST

When the fruit is very ripe, the outer skin will begin to crack. When you start seeing cracks, it is your cue to harvest all the fruit, both cracked and uncracked. Snip the fruit off the branch, or cut the entire branch to use inside for decoration.

Pomegranate fruits can be stored for up to 3 months in the refrigerator if kept whole. To harvest its seeds, score the bottom with an X and push on the X to break the pomegranate open without breaking open the seeds. You can also simply cut the fruit in half, but this will release some of the seeds' highly staining juice. Each mature fruit can contain 200 to 1,400 seeds. Seed the pomegranate into a bowl of cold water. The white, pithy membrane will float to the top and the seeds will sink to the bottom. Scoop the pith out of the bowl, strain the seeds, and add them to salads or add the juice to sparkling water or cocktails. To juice the seeds, place them in a sealable plastic bag and run a rolling pin over the bag. Then cut a corner of the bag and pour off the juice. Pomegranate juice can be preserved by freezing for up to a year.

POMEGRANATE MARGARITA

MAKES 4 DRINKS

1 cup of your favorite tequila

1 cup triple sec

½ cup fresh pomegranate juice (from about 2 pomegranates)

½ cup fresh lime juice

Large-grained salt such as kosher or flake salt

Lime slice

Ice cubes

Handful of pomegranate seeds, for garnish

Classic cocktail meets holiday tradition, compliments of Stefani's mom, Garna, who took the margarita and dressed it with a splash of festive red. Whether you are making a single glass or a pitcher, the ratio of the ingredients stays the same. Use more lime juice if you prefer a tart margarita or more pomegranate juice if you prefer it sweeter.

———

Combine the tequila, triple sec, and both juices in a pitcher and stir thoroughly. Pour the salt onto a small plate. Rub the lime slice around the rim of each glass, and then dip the rims in the salt. Pour the margarita over ice in the salt-rimmed glasses. For a seasonal festive touch, garnish with the pomegranate seeds.

MASHUA
Tropaeolum tuberosum

_____

One of the great joys of growing your own food is that it creates the opportunity to try unique, lesser-known fruits and vegetables that you would never find at the local grocery store. Mashua is a perfect example. Its ubiquitous cousin, the easy-to-grow nasturtium, is one of the most well-known edible flowers out there, and, as with nasturtium, you can eat mashua leaves, flowers, and seeds. Mashua's main crop, however, is its tubers.

If you're looking for a delicious alternative to potatoes, mashua is the answer. Its tubers are long and come in a variety of colors, and they can be roasted, baked, fried, and cooked in soups and stews.

IN THE GARDEN

Mashua is one of the easiest salad plants you can grow. A hardy perennial in USDA zones 7 to 10, it can be grown in all zones if you dig up the tubers and bring them indoors during the winter months, similar to how you'd overwinter a dahlia. Mashua is absolutely worth planting no matter what your growing zone.

This climber grows 7 to 13 feet (2 to 4 m), producing masses of lush, rounded, blue-green foliage and trumpet-shaped, orange-red flowers. Bloom time is midsummer throughout fall until frost.

Plant tubers once the threat of frost has passed, usually in March. Start seed indoors about 3 months before you move them outside. In mild climates, mashua prefers full sun. In warmer climates, it will grow best with some afternoon shade. Mashua can grow in almost any type of garden soil as long as it's kept moist. In our Mediterranean climate, we plant it in our kitchen gardens instead of the lower-water landscape. For those of you with summer rain, try adding it to a space where it can climb with support.

HARVEST

Mashua tubers form near the surface and are typically harvested when the plant's leaves and flowers die back after a winter frost. When harvesting the tubers and roots, make sure that you don't spear the crop with your garden fork or shovel. Gently harvest the tubers using a hand trowel and your hands. Tubers can reach up to 13 inches (33 cm) in length.

Where mashua can overwinter outside, harvest some for eating and allow others to remain in the ground to grow again the following year. In cooler zones, store a portion of the harvest to plant in the garden the following spring.

All parts of the mashua plant can be eaten raw or cooked. The leaves and tubers have a mild, peppery taste, reminiscent of radish. Larger leaves can be used to wrap other ingredients, similar to grape leaves but with a spicy kick. The blooms are a go-to late edible flower in all of our salads, which we can use much longer than less cold-hardy greens. Mashua tubers are high in vitamin C and relatively high in protein for a root crop. Although you can eat them raw, we prefer to cook them or use them to make pickles.

TUBER MASH

Mashua grows underground like a potato, but the aboveground vine looks like a nasturtium. Its tubers taste a bit like anise and are packed full of nutrients. Developed in the Andean mountains in South America, this root vegetable is best served mashed with butter and seasoned with sea salt and pepper. If you have no parsnips on hand and extra mashua, simply omit the parsnips and double the mashua.

MAKES 4 SERVINGS

¾ pound mashua tubers

¾ pound parsnips

1½ pounds Yukon gold potatoes

Kosher or sea salt

2 tablespoons unsalted organic butter, melted

1 tablespoon chopped fresh parsley

1 tablespoon chopped fresh chives

⅛ teaspoon freshly ground black pepper

Wash the mashua tubers, and wash and peel the parsnips and potatoes. Cut the parsnips and potatoes crosswise into ½-inch (1.3-cm) thick medallions. Place them all into a medium saucepan, cover with water, and add 2 teaspoons salt. Bring to a simmer, lower the heat, cover, and let simmer for 10 minutes, until a fork easily pierces the vegetables.

Drain off the water, and remove the pan from the heat. Return the mashua, parsnips, and potatoes to the warm pan. Cover, and let the vegetables steam in the heat of the pan for 10 minutes. Add the melted butter and ½ teaspoon salt. Using a potato masher or hand mixer, mash the vegetables. There's no need to mash them completely smooth; some small pieces add a nice texture and flavor to the dish. Stir in the chopped parsley and chives. Add the black pepper and season with salt before serving.

CALENDULA
Calendula officinalis

Calendula is one of our favorite flowers in the winter and early spring. Its bright flowers are edible and medicinal. Calendula is prolific on many levels: color, abundance of blooms, and nutritional value. With open-faced flowers similar to daisies, calendula comes in double- and single-head varieties in a rich kaleidoscope of colors.

IN THE GARDEN

Easy to grow from seeds or seedlings, this lovely annual will bloom from spring to winter. Calendula is not fussy about soil type as long as the soil is moist and well draining. In most areas, it prefers full sun or partial shade.

Calendula is one of the easiest ornamental edibles to add to your garden, whether it's planted in a container or planting bed. The plant has an upright growth habit of 18 to 24 inches (46 to 60 cm) tall, so you can tuck it in among other plants. We love the more unusual types, including 'Strawberry Blonde', 'Bronzed Beauty', 'Radio', and cultivars in the 'Flashback Series'.

HARVEST

Harvest calendula flowers and add the petals to salads and herb butters for an instant pop of color; sprinkle them on as generously as you'd like. Calendula makes a beautiful natural dye, and because it has healing powers, you can use the flower heads or petals to make your own tinctures and oils, and as the basis of a medicinal herbal tea.

Flowers can be dried by various means, including air drying or in a dehydrator. Fully dried flowers can be stored in a sealed container for up to 3 months.

CALENDULA-INFUSED ESSENTIAL OIL

Sore muscles appreciate a little calendula oil. Use calendula to create a fantastic medicinal topical oil for massage and for soothing dry skin or light skin injuries. It can also be the basis for herbal salves and lip balms.

———

Fill a 1-pint jar halfway full with the calendula flowers. Top off the jar with the olive oil, covering the flowers. Place a lid on the jar and store in a cool, dark place for 3 to 4 weeks. Check on the oil occasionally and give it a vigorous shake.

MAKES 1 PINT

10 to 15 fresh or dried calendula flowers

2 cups all-purpose olive oil (cold-pressed or extra-virgin oil is not required)

Once infused, strain the oil into a second jar. Press or squeeze the flower heads or petals through a strainer to release the remaining infused oil. Do not be concerned if you have less oil than when you started; the petals will have absorbed some of the oil. Seal with a lid and store the infusion in a cool, dark place. It should keep for a year.

PROJECT INGREDIENT ALTERNATIVES

Most of the projects in this book are highly versatile and can be made with many different kinds of plants. Here are our suggestions for alternatives. The main plant or plants for each project are indicated in italic.

PROJECT	PLANTS
Bitters (page 94)	alpine strawberry, anise hyssop, bachelor's buttons, 'Berggarten' sage, blackberry, blueberry, borage, calamintha, calendula, chinotto orange, elderberry/elderflower, flowering basils, *gem marigolds*, huckleberry, lavender, lemon bee balm, lilac, mashua, oregano, rose, rosemary, scented geranium, thyme, viola
Blooming butter (page 26)	amaranth, anise hyssop, *bachelor's buttons*, 'Berggarten' sage, borage, calendula, flowering basils, gem marigolds, lavender, lemon bee balm, lilac, mashua flowers, oregano, peppermint candy flower, rose, rosemary, scented geranium, shungiku, thyme, viola
Edible flower garnish (page 182)	alpine strawberry flower, amaranth, anise hyssop, bachelor's buttons, 'Berggarten' sage flower, *borage*, calendula, chinotto orange flower, dwarf winter savory, flowering basils, gem marigolds, lavender, lemon bee balm, lilac, mashua flowers, oregano flowers, peppermint candy flower, pineapple guava flower, rose, rosemary flowers, scented geranium, shungiku flowers, thyme flower, viola
Edible flower–pressed cheese (page 38)	alpine strawberry flowers, anise hyssop, bachelor's buttons, 'Berggarten' sage flowers, borage, calamintha, flowering basils, gem marigolds, lavender, lemon bee balm, lilac, mashua flowers, oregano, *peppermint candy flower*, purple coneflower, rose, rosemary flowers, shungiku flowers, viola
Garden arrangement (pages 22, 34, 74, 90, 110, 166)	*alpine strawberry*, *apple/crabapple*, *artichoke/cardoon*, *blackberry*, *Chilean guava*, *flowering basils*, and all plants in this book
Gardener's salve (page 78)	anise hyssop, 'Berggarten' sage, calendula, chinotto orange, feverfew, lavender, lemon bee balm, lilac, *purple coneflower*, rose, rosemary, scented geranium
Herbs preserved in salt (page 134)	anise hyssop, 'Berggarten' sage, calendula, *dwarf winter savory*, lavender, oregano, rose, rosemary, thyme
Infused essential oil (page 202)	anise hyssop, bay laurel, 'Berggarten' sage, borage, calamintha, *calendula*, dwarf winter savory, feverfew, gem marigolds, lavender, lemon bee balm, lilac, mashua, oregano, purple coneflower, rose, rosemary, scented geranium, thyme, viola, yarrow
Infused honey (page 42)	apricot, blackberry, *elderflower*, huckleberry, lavender, lilac, pomegranate, rhubarb, rose
Infused vinegar (page 66)	anise hyssop, bay laurel, 'Berggarten' sage, borage, calendula, dwarf winter savory, flowering basils, gem marigolds, lavender, lilac, mashua, *oregano*, rose, rosemary, thyme, viola, yarrow
Infused water (page 178)	alpine strawberry, anise hyssop, apricot, Australian finger lime, blackberry, blueberry, borage, calamintha, calendula, chinotto orange, elderberry/elderflower, flowering basils, gem marigolds, huckleberry, lavender, lemon bee balm, lemongrass, lilac, mashua, pineapple guava, pomegranate, rose, rosemary, scented geranium, turmeric, *viola*, yarrow
Lip balm (page 126)	alpine strawberry, anise hyssop, blackberry, blueberry, borage, *calamintha*, calendula, chinotto orange, elderberry/elderflower, gem marigolds, huckleberry, lavender, lemon bee balm, lemongrass, lilac, pomegranate, purple coneflower, rose, rosemary, scented geranium, thyme

PROJECT	PLANTS
Plant dye (pages 86, 174)	alpine strawberry, amaranth, artichoke/cardoon, Asian persimmon, bachelor's buttons, 'Berggarten' sage, blackberry, *blueberry*, borage, calendula, chinotto orange, elderberry, flowering basils, gem marigolds, huckleberry, lavender, lemon bee balm, lemongrass, lilac, mashua, oregano, pomegranate, purple coneflower, quince, rhubarb, rose, rosemary, thyme, *turmeric*, viola, yarrow
Preserves: jams, jellies & paste (page 142)	alpine strawberry, apple/crabapple, Australian finger lime, blackberry, blueberry, Chilean guava, chinotto orange, elderberry, huckleberry, lavender, lilac, pineapple guava, pomegranate, *quince*, rhubarb, rose
Salt scrub (page 98)	apricot, calendula, chinotto orange, lavender, *lemongrass*, rose, rosemary, scented geranium, thyme
Scented sugar (page 62)	anise hyssop, borage, chinotto orange, elderflower, flowering basils, lavender, lemongrass, lilac, rose, rosemary, *scented geranium*, thyme
Seasonal herb salad (pages 30, 118, 158)	alpine strawberry, *amaranth*, anise hyssop, bachelor's buttons, 'Berggarten' sage, black cumin seed, borage, breadseed poppy seed, calamintha, calendula, dwarf winter savory, flowering basils, gem marigolds, lavender, lemon bee balm, lilac, mashua, oregano, peppermint candy flower, pineapple guava flowers, rose, rosemary flowers, *salad burnet*, *shungiku*, thyme, viola
Shrub (page 130)	apple/crabapple, apricot, Asian persimmon, blackberry, blueberry, chinotto orange, elderberry, *huckleberry*, pineapple guava, pomegranate, quince, rhubarb
Simple syrup (page 150)	alpine strawberry, anise hyssop, apricot, Australian finger lime, bay laurel, 'Berggarten' sage, blackberry, blueberry, borage, Chilean guava, chinotto orange, elderberry, flowering basils, gem marigolds, huckleberry, lavender, lemon bee balm, lemongrass, lilac, oregano, *pineapple guava*, pomegranate, quince, rhubarb, rose, rosemary, scented geranium, thyme
Smudge sticks (page 190)	'Berggarten' sage, lavender, rose, *rosemary*, thyme
Tea (pages 50, 70, 82, 114)	alpine strawberry, *anise hyssop*, 'Berggarten' sage, blackberry, black cumin, calamintha, calendula, Chilean guava, chinotto orange, elderflower, *feverfew*, flowering basils, gem marigolds, *lavender*, *lemon bee balm*, lemongrass, lilac, oregano, purple coneflower, rhubarb, rose, rosemary, scented geranium, thyme, viola, yarrow
Tincture (page 106)	calendula, elderberry, feverfew, lavender, lemongrass, lilac, oregano, purple coneflower, rose, rosemary, turmeric, *yarrow*
Wreath & garland (pages 146, 154, 186)	*Asian persimmon, bay laurel, 'Berggarten' sage*, feverfew, lavender, oregano, pomegranate, quince, rosemary, thyme, yarrow

TERMS & TECHNIQUES

Here is more in-depth information about some of the terms and techniques that we reference throughout the book.

DRYING HERBS, EDIBLE FLOWERS, AND CITRUS

Bundle harvested herbs and edible flowers with a rubber band or wrap with a piece of twine, and then hang the bundles in a space with good air circulation and away from direct sunlight. The plants will typically dry in 2 weeks. To test for dryness, touch the herbs or flowers. When they are dry to the touch and crumble easily, the drying process is complete. If the herb or flower is still pliable and bends easily, continue to let it dry. Once dried, remove the leaves and/or whole flower heads from the stems—if you are using only petals, remove the petals from the flower centers. Store dried material in a clean, dry jar. Dried herbs or flowers will keep for a year.

Other drying methods include using a dehydrator, a fantastic tool for preserving herbs, edible flowers, and fruits. Dehydrators are easy to use and typically come with instructions on how to use the equipment and drying times. Citrus can also be dehydrated by slicing thinly, laying on a parchment-lined baking sheet, and placing in a 200°F (94°C) oven for 5 to 6 hours until dry.

DYEING 101

Cotton and linen fabrics require a fixative, such as salt, to help set the dye so that your creation does not lose its color. As a rule, use 1 part salt to 16 parts water.

You prepare the fabric for dyeing by simmering it in a saltwater bath. This step will help the fabric better absorb the dye so that it will hold the color through multiple washings. All dyed fabrics should be laundered only in cold water to preserve their color.

Before you get started, keep in mind that all kitchen supplies, such as pots, that are used in the dyeing process should not be used for cooking food.

OVERWINTERING PLANTS INDOORS

Many of the plants we love to grow are perennial for folks in some gardening zones and annuals for others. If you happen to live in a part of the world with particularly cold winters, you may need to bring more tender plants indoors during winter months if you want them to be more than annuals. The key is to make sure that the plants are accessible and easily moved indoors—typically, this means container plantings. If you want to grow citrus or other large plants in a pot, go easy on your back and use a container dolly under the pot to wheel the container indoors and outdoors.

PRUNING FRUIT TREES

Many deciduous fruit trees require pruning to stimulate new fruiting wood (the branches that produce the flowers that make the fruit), to remove misshapen or diseased wood, to control tree size, and to allow good air circulation between branches. Pruning is most important in the first three years after planting, because this is when the shape and size of a fruit tree are established.

Fruit trees can be winter and summer pruned. We prune our trees in the winter to stimulate new fruiting wood and make branch corrections, and we prune in the summer to control tree size. Think of it this way: In the winter, pruning stimulates growth, and in the summer, it restricts it. We believe that fruit trees should be kept at manageable, harvestable heights in the garden, usually from 4 to 8 feet (1.2 to 2.4 m) tall. Summer pruning is the key. It's much easier (on you and the tree) to keep a small tree small than to make a large tree small.

SUCCESSION PLANTING

Succession planting is a gardening technique used to ensure a continuous harvest throughout the year. This means that we grow plants with early-, mid-, and late-season harvest times. As one plant stops fruiting or flowering, the next one begins. This will provide smaller, continuous harvests throughout the year instead of just one that is large and overwhelming. Different varieties of the same plant can have different harvest times. For example, apple trees can produce fruit from early July to November, depending on the variety. If you love apples and want to eat them out of the garden for longer than just a few weeks, include multiple trees in your garden, including one with an early harvest, another with a midseason harvest, and a third with a late harvest.

WINTER CHILL HOURS

Winter chill hours refers to the number of winter hours in which temperatures are 32°F to 45°F (0°C to 7°C) that certain plants require in order to produce fruit or flowers. Choosing plants appropriate to your garden's climate and number of winter chill hours helps ensure that your plants are more productive.

RESOURCES

BARE-ROOT FRUIT TREES

Peaceful Valley
Farm & Garden Supply
www.groworganic.com

Trees of Antiquity
www.treesofantiquity.com

BEESWAX, AMBER JARS, AND LIP BALM CONTAINERS

Mountain Rose Herbs
www.mountainroseherbs.com

CERAMIC VESSELS, FERMENTATION JARS, AND BOWLS

Colleen Hennessey
www.colleenhennessey.net

Heath Ceramics
www.heathceramics.com

Sarah Kersten
www.sarahkersten.com

CITRUS PLANTS

Four Winds Growers
www.fourwindsgrowers.com

HERB AND EDIBLE FLOWER PLANTS

Annie's Annuals & Perennials
www.anniesannuals.com

Morningsun Herb Farm
www.morningsunherbfarm.com

MASHUA TUBERS

Cultivariable
www.cultivariable.com

NATURAL PLANT DYE RESOURCES

Dharma Trading Company
www.dharmatrading.com

A Verb for Keeping Warm
www.averbforkeepingwarm.com

PADDLE WIRE, WREATH RINGS, AND OTHER FLORAL ACCESSORIES

Shibata Floral Company
www.shibatafloral.com

RHUBARB AND ARTICHOKE CROWNS

Peaceful Valley
Farm & Garden Supply
www.groworganic.com

SEEDS

Adaptive Seeds
www.adaptiveseeds.com

Baker Creek Heirloom Seeds
www.rareseeds.com

Fedco Seeds
www.fedcoseeds.com

Johnny's Selected Seeds
www.johnnyseeds.com

Kitazawa Seed Company
www.kitazawaseed.com
(shungiku seeds)

Larner Seeds
www.larnerseeds.com
(peppermint candy flower seeds)

Territorial Seed Company
www.territorialseed.com

Uprising Seeds
uprisingorganics.com
(black cumin seeds)

TURMERIC RHIZOMES AND PLANTS

Asparagus Gardener
store.asparagusgardener.com

Plant Delights Nursery
www.plantdelights.com

USDA HARDINESS ZONES

USDA Plant Hardiness Zone Map
www.planthardiness.ars.usda.gov/PHZMWeb

ACKNOWLEDGMENTS

We are grateful to the wonderful garden-loving people in our lives who helped *Harvest* come into being. First and foremost, David Fenton, our partner in this project—thank you, David, for your humor, patience, skill, and friendship. This book would not be the same without your beautiful photography. Thanks also to our agent, Andrea Barvzi of Empire Literary, for her support and advocacy, and Paul Cannon, for helping us with initial copyediting and writing and for helping us create a story. Debra Prinzing, founder of the Slow Flowers movement and mentor—thank you for your support and kind words. Thanks to Mary Ann Newcomer, our zone expert who made sure that our California love of plants was relatable for those in other zones; all the folks at Ten Speed Press, especially our editor Lisa Regul and art director Ashley Lima; and the crew at Homestead Design Collective, our edible landscaping firm in the San Francisco Bay Area. And thank you to our clients who shared their gardens for this project—the Stengers, Cottrills, Klines, and McCoys. Thanks to our moms, Garna and Kay, who both inspire our love of gardens, food, and flowers; and our husbands, Jay and Chris, and kids, Ana, Lauren, Max, Alejandra, and Ever, who we do this with and for.

INDEX

—
W

—
Y

Published in the United States by Ten Speed Press, an imprint of the
Crown Publishing Group, a division of Penguin Random House LLC, New York.
www.crownpublishing.com
www.tenspeed.com

Ten Speed Press and the Ten Speed Press colophon are registered
trademarks of Penguin Random House LLC.

Library of Congress Cataloging-in-Publication Data
Names: Bittner, Stefani, 1969- author. | Harampolis, Alethea.
Title: Harvest : unexpected projects using 47 extraordinary garden plants /
    Stefani Bittner & Alethea Harampolis ; photography by David Fenton.
Description: First edition. | Berkeley : Ten Speed Press, [2017] | Includes
    bibliographical references and index.
Identifiers: LCCN 2016029813 (print) | LCCN 2016037529 (ebook)
Subjects: LCSH: Cooking (Herbs) | Flower arrangement. | Herbal cosmetics. |
    Medicinal plants. | Plant products. | Gardening.
Classification: LCC TX819.H4 B58 2017 (print) | LCC TX819.H4 (ebook) | DDC
    641.6/57—dc23
LC record available at https://lccn.loc.gov/2016029813

Hardcover ISBN: 978-0-399-57833-5
eBook ISBN: 978-0-399-57834-2

Printed in China

Design by Ashley Lima

10 9 8 7 6 5 4 3 2 1

First Edition